Passionate readers both, Olivia Langdon and Mark Twain courted through books, spelling out their expectations through literary references as they corresponded during their frequent separations. Their letters reveal Olivia Langdon not as a Victorian prude, as many twentieth-century critics have portrayed her, but as a thoughtful intellectual, widely read in literature, history, and modern science. Not surprisingly, the letters show Twain as a critic, a suitor who lampooned Langdon's interests even while he sought to win her love. While Langdon's letters show her carefully considering her culture's array of possible role models, Twain's exhibit his conservatism about women's nature and roles. At the same time, they show him resisting many of his culture's basic assumptions. Working with Langdon's own letters and diaries as well as Twain's, Harris traces the complexities of Langdon and Twain's courtship within their larger contexts, showing how they negotiated their relationship through the mediums of literature, material culture, and the dynamics of the extended family.

CAMBRIDGE STUDIES IN AMERICAN LITERATURE AND CULTURE

The Courtship of Olivia Langdon and Mark Twain

Continued on pages following the Index

THE COURTSHIP OF OLIVIA LANGDON AND MARK TWAIN

SUSAN K. HARRIS
Pennsylvania State University

CAMBRIDGE
UNIVERSITY PRESS

Published by the Press Syndicate of the University of Cambridge
The Pitt Building, Trumpington Street, Cambridge CB2 1RP
40 West 20th Street, New York, NY 10011-4211, USA
10 Stamford Road, Oakleigh, Melbourne 3166, Australia

© Cambridge University Press 1996

First published 1996

Printed in the United States of America

Library of Congress Cataloging-in-Publication Data
Harris, Susan K., 1945–
The courtship of Olivia Langdon and Mark Twain / Susan K. Harris.
p.   cm. – (Cambridge studies in American literature and
culture : 101)
Includes bibliographical references and index.
ISBN 0-521-55384-8 (hardcover). – ISBN 0-521-55650-3 (pbk.)
1. Twain, Mark, 1835–1910 – Biography – Marriage.   2. Courtship –
United States – History – 19th century.   3. Clemens, Olivia Langdon,
1845–1904 – Marriage.   4. Authors, American – 19th century – Biography.
5. Authors' spouses – United States – Biography.   I. Title.
II. Series.
PS1332.H375   1996
818'.409 – dc20   96-31990
[B]   CIP

A catalog record for this book is available from the British Library.

ISBN 0-521-55384-9 hardback
ISBN 0-521-55650-3 paperback

Dedicated to the memory of Darryl Baskin,
first director of the Elmira Center
for Mark Twain Studies at Quarry Farm

CONTENTS

ACKNOWLEDGMENTS

━━━━━━━━

I have dedicated this book to the memory of Darryl Baskin because his interest in Elmira history was directly responsible for its inception. I first visited the Elmira Center for Mark Twain Studies at Quarry Farm in 1988. Though I had published a book on Twain in the early 1980s, I had moved away from Mark Twain studies and did not think I would ever return. But Darryl was searching for speakers for the center's lecture series, and someone gave him my name. I flew to Elmira and Darryl picked me up at the airport. On the way to the farm he lectured me on Elmira's demography, past and present. I remember that ride as a kaleidoscope through local history, a series of historical juxtapositions. By the time we reached the farm I wanted to know more. Over the next few years I returned to the area several times to explore its possibilities. By 1992, when the National Endowment for the Humanities granted me a fellowship to research a study of Olivia Langdon's reading, I knew I was hooked.

In the course of researching and writing this book I have incurred more debts than ever before. Most important is my debt to Quarry Farm itself. One of scholars' few perks is the occasional chance to actually live in a historical house, and I know that I speak for many members of the Mark Twain community when I say that for me staying at Quarry Farm has been among the most moving experiences of my life. At this writing, I have been acquainted with the house for seven years, and it has become a part of my life – tranquil mornings in the study or on the porch, stormy nights in the kitchen or parlor, the memory of my daughter's eighth birthday celebrated on the lawn, the thought of our Brooklyn-born cat, ecstatic at being brought out of the city for the summer, killed on the road and buried with a hundred other cats in the area behind the barn. Over the years, I have come to know the ghosts who so kindly keep alive the past embodied here, and I thank them for succoring me and mine as they succored so many refugees from the furious pace of our American lives.

But my debts are not only to the dead. In historical studies the present makes the past possible, and that is hard work. Darryl Baskin's sudden death in 1992 was made bearable only by the leadership of Gretchen Sharlow, currently director of the center. Gretchen's energy, dedication, and scholarship have been invaluable, and her humor has sustained us all. With Gretchen, the rest of the Elmira Center staff – from Mark Woodhouse, the librarian at the Mark Twain Archives in Elmira College's Gannett-Tripp Library, to former caretaker Gail Early and current caretaker Karen Ernhout – has made this study possible. To all of them I owe my heartfelt thanks.

Many other people and institutions have helped me on my way. Bob Hirst, head of the Mark Twain Project at Berkeley, has as always been a strong support and guide, sending me materials and making himself accessible as he has done for so many researchers. He is an outstanding scholar and a dedicated director, and I sincerely think that the project is one of the great editing feats of the century. Marianne Curling, at the Mark Twain Memorial in Hartford, has also advised, corrected, and counseled me, and to her I send many thanks. To the staffs at the Watkinson Library at Trinity College, where the Hartford collection of Twain materials is currently housed, and at the Stowe-Day Library, where I have spent many hours researching this and other projects, I am deeply grateful. These four major collections – at Elmira, at Berkeley, at Trinity, and at Stowe-Day – have shown me once again how inestimable is the value of librarians and curators. A collection is only as good as the staff that cares for it.

I am indebted to other people and institutions as well: to the

Chemung County Historical Society; the Steele Memorial Public Library in Elmira; the research division of the New York Public Library, particularly the Wertheim Room, reserved for scholars; to Charles Mann and Sandy Stelts of the rare books room at Penn State University's Pattee Library. And to the granting agencies that supported released time for this project: the National Endowment for the Humanities, for a faculty fellowship for 1992-3, and Penn State's Research and Graduate Studies Office for a course release for the fall 1995 semester. I also want to thank Robert Secor, former head of Penn State's English Department, for his support since I joined the faculty in 1992.

Finally but not least, I am indebted to the friends who – unpaid – have read this manuscript and encouraged me to improve it. My first reader was Howard Kumin, my father, who read it while it was very much in draft and urged me to make it more accessible to general readers. My second reader, a year later, was Joan Hedrick, whose acute criticisms of what I had hoped was my final draft stimulated three more months of revisions, aimed both at making the text still more accessible and at clarifying my concepts and expanding cultural contexts. Both Gretchen Sharlow and the reader for Cambridge University Press corrected factual errors. My friend Bonnie Stretch, herself an editor, and my friend and colleague Ann Carter Rose combed the manuscript for style. Shannon Nichols helped me prepare the manuscript for publication, and Chris Weinmann cheerfully undertook the indexing. At the last moment, when I was struggling with the copyedited version on a trip abroad, Terry Webster, of Murdoch University in Western Australia, provided me with sorely needed advice and encouragement. To all these kind friends I am deeply indebted. Whatever factual errors remain, whatever lapses of grace are evident, are wholly my own responsibility.

Finally – but no, I have already said "finally." To the bedrock, the basis, the field of possibility for all my work, I thank Billy Joe and Kate, for their love and support and for simply being there.

Quarry Farm, May 16, 1995

A NOTE ABOUT NAMES

Some readers may be disturbed by my referring to Olivia Louise Langdon Clemens as "Langdon" throughout this book. I do so because I find it offensively familiar for biographers and critics to refer to their subjects by first name. Additionally, when the subject is a woman, calling her by her first name is both patronizing and denigrating. On principle, then, I do not use first names alone.

I also realize, however, that my principles occasionally entail confusion, largely because women's last names change. Many women are also happy to be known by their husbands' surnames. Nevertheless, for consistency's sake, I have decided to stick to "Langdon" even after Olivia Langdon becomes Olivia Clemens. One of the few places I bend this rule is in sections of Chapter 5, where I discuss the Clemenses' first child, Langdon Clemens. There I refer to him as "baby Langdon" and to his mother as "Olivia."

INTRODUCTION

―――――

Olivia Louise Langdon was Jervis and Olivia Lewis Langdon's first biological child, born on November 27, 1845, in the fourteenth year of her parents' marriage.[1] Her sister Susan, born in 1836, had been adopted early in Susan's childhood;[2] her biological brother Charles would be born in 1849.[3]

At the time of Langdon's birth her parents had lived in Elmira only one year. Through the course of a career that began with shopkeeping in a succession of upstate New York towns and ended with a modest coal empire, Jervis Langdon had become involved with the lumber business, and had come to Elmira in 1845 to establish a lumber company in partnership with Sylvester G. Andrus. The business prospered; the partners invested in coal as well as lumber, operating mines not only in New York's Southern Tier but also in northern Pennsylvania. By 1860 the Elmira census listed Jervis Langdon, then age 51, as having real estate valued at $92,000 and a personal estate valued at $50,000.[4] Although this did not put him in a league with Jay Gould, it did ensure his family a comfortable living. In the early 1860s the Langdons moved from the modest house in which Olivia Louise had been born and reared to a mansion built the previous decade by the late Anson C. Ely, one of the organizers of the local bank.[5] Most of 1866 was spent renovating the new house, including installing a furnace and a water closet, and creating a conservatory that opened out from the dining room.[6] By the time Samuel

1

Clemens appeared on the scene in 1868, the Langdons were established as one of the leading families in town.

The Langdon seniors were committed to social progress and human equality in addition to material success. During the 1830s, when they lived in Millport, about twenty miles from Elmira and at that time a thriving lumber and boat-building town on the Chemung Canal, they may have been involved with the Underground Railroad.[7] At the very least, they lodged Frederick Douglass, a known fugitive slave, on one of his lecturing trips through the region, and as letters from him document, continued to offer him hospitality when he was in the Elmira area.[8] In an era when few whites, even "liberal" ones, felt sufficiently comfortable with African Americans to socialize with them as equals, putting a black man in the guest room and welcoming him to the breakfast and dinner table was no mean sign of courage and commitment. In a further demonstration of that commitment, the Langdons were among the parishioners who separated from the Presbyterian Church in 1846 when it refused to condemn slavery. Founding members of the Independent Congregational Church (later the Park Congregational Church), they were intimate friends of Thomas K. Beecher, a theological radical, and Julia Beecher, his feminist wife. Although no documentation can be found to substantiate it, local lore insists that during their years in Elmira prior to the Civil War, Jervis and Olivia Lewis Langdon, with their friends Thomas K. Beecher, James M. Robinson, William Yates, and Riggs Watrous, were financial backers of the branch of the Underground Railroad that came through Elmira and that was "conducted" by ex-slave John W. Jones.[9] Certainly during these and subsequent years they were host to such inflammatory visitors as William Lloyd Garrison, Wendell Phillips, and Gerrit Smith.[10] Jervis Langdon was also an early supporter of Elmira College, the first U.S. college to be chartered to grant the baccalaureate to women.[11] As one sign of their support for the college, he and his wife moved their daughter Olivia from the excellent school that she had been attending to the college's preparatory branch.

Despite her parents' wealth and social commitments and the

apparently harmonious relations among her family, Olivia Louise Langdon's adolescence was not without trial. A slow, unspecified illness consumed the years that she and her parents expected to be devoted to education. In 1860, when she was fourteen, she was apparently sufficiently debilitated to be placed in residence at the Elmira Water Cure, a well-known hydropathy establishment about two miles from her home. Run by Drs. Silas O. and Rachel Brooks Gleason, the Water Cure attracted men and women famous and obscure; our knowledge of Langdon's stint there is indebted to a letter from her roommate, Isabella Beecher Hooker, who came to the cure from her home in Hartford, Connecticut. For Langdon, however, the Water Cure did not succeed, and she spent the majority of the next six years in various sanitariums in Washington, D.C., and New York City.

Mark Twain legend – possibly invented and certainly perpetrated by Twain himself – has it that Langdon fell on the ice at the age of sixteen, was paralyzed, and spent two years in bed until a faith healer "raised" her in 1864. Laura Skandera has recently traced Langdon's movements and treatments during these years and has hypothesized that she had contracted Potts Disease, a paralysis of the spine, for which she was finally successfully treated by homeopathic doctors Charles and George Taylor at their well-known clinic in New York City.[12] It is clear from her mother's diary that Langdon lived in New York City for a time without her family, and that by 1866 she had returned home, where she was steadily, if slowly, gaining strength. Her commonplace book, which she began while she was at the Taylors' clinic, gives some indication of her interests during her time in therapy; after 1866 her mother's diary, as well as Langdon's own letters to her friend Alice Hooker, and Hooker's letters to *her* mother Isabella, indicate that much of Langdon's energy was devoted to catching up on both the education and the social life she had missed during her years in the sanitariums. By the time she met Clemens in New York City late in 1867 she was sufficiently recovered to join her family for their winter shopping and theater spree, but she was easily fatigued and still prone to rest in the family suite at the St.

3

Nicholas Hotel more than the others. She would be known as delicate and susceptible to disease the rest of her life; in the midst of her delicacy, however, she managed to bear four children, run a complex household, entertain lavishly, and do a considerable amount of journeying around the world.

Samuel Langhorne Clemens's early biography is much better known than his wife's and needs little recapitulation here. Born on November 30, 1835 in Florida, Missouri, member of a large and at times tragic family, he spent his childhood in Hannibal, thirty miles from his birthplace, on the Mississippi River. Clemens's father, John Marshall Clemens, was like Jervis Langdon in keeping shop; he was unlike him in being largely unsuccessful. After his death in 1847, Clemens's brother Orion, a printer, largely supported the family, while their mother, Jane Lampton Clemens, took in boarders and the other family members chipped in.

Clemens's formal schooling, never very consistent, ended in 1849. In 1848 he began to learn the printer's trade; in 1851 he went to work for Orion, and over the next few years he wrote and printed his first humorous sketches. By 1855 the entire Clemens family had left Hannibal: brother Orion to go to Keokuk, Iowa, home of his new wife, Mollie Stotts, where he set up a print shop and briefly employed Sam; sister Pamela, now married to William Moffett, to St. Louis, where their mother, Jane Lampton Clemens, and presumably their younger brother Henry, joined her. In 1857 Clemens apprenticed himself to steamboat pilot Horace Bixby; receiving his license early in 1859, he successfully piloted the Mississippi until 1861, when fear that he would be impressed by Union forces motivated him to enlist in the Confederate volunteers.

Clemens's stint in the military lasted two weeks. After crawling about the countryside searching for battles (in order, he later claimed, to avoid them) his troop disbanded and Clemens accepted a job as Orion's secretary when that peripatetic sibling decided to move to Nevada to work for the territorial governor. Over the succeeding seven years Samuel Clemens's horizons broadened and Mark Twain was born. Clemens's assignment to Orion's staff lasted no longer than any of his previous jobs with his brother. After it ended Clemens spent part of his time learning how to be a miner, more of it speculating in mining stock, and the most useful part of it learning how to write. Beginning as a correspondent for several western papers, he at one point rose to the position of staff reporter for the *Territorial Enterprise*. Living in a boom/bust economy, he followed its customs, alternating between boarding houses in the territories and luxurious hotels in San Francisco. Though he had been using pseudonyms since 1852, he first signed letters "Mark Twain" early in 1863. During this period he also began to publish in eastern papers; "Jim Smiley and His Jumping Frog" was reprinted throughout the country. In 1866 – the year Olivia Langdon returned home from her years in sanitariums – he traveled to the Sandwich Islands (Hawaii) as a correspondent for the Sacramento *Union*; in addition to the newspaper letters that resulted, this trip also launched his lecturing career, when he developed a series of highly successful talks about the islands after his return. In 1867 Clemens returned to the East, edited his first collection of sketches (*The Celebrated Jumping Frog of Calaveras County and Other Sketches*), lectured on the Sandwich Islands, and engaged to be the correspondent for the New York *Tribune*, the New York *Herald*, and the *Alta California* on the first organized tour from the United States to Europe and the Holy Land. The *Quaker City*, the ship chartered for the jaunt, left New York in June; one of its passengers was Olivia Langdon's brother Charles, whom Mark Twain would befriend on the boat and later immortalize in *The Innocents Abroad* as "the Interrogation Point." Returning to the States in November, he worked briefly in Washington, D.C., and contracted with the American Publishing Company in Hartford, Connecticut, to turn his *Quaker City* letters into a book. In December he visited New York, where Charles Langdon introduced him to his family at their suite in the St. Nicholas Hotel. That night the entire group went to hear Charles Dickens read.

The Courtship of Olivia Langdon and Mark Twain began as a study

Jervis Langdon, c. 1869. The Mark Twain Project, The Bancroft Library, University of California at Berkeley.

Olivia Lewis Langdon, c. 1870. The Mark Twain Project, The Bancroft Library, University of California at Berkeley.

Olivia Louise Langdon, *c.* 1857. The Mark Twain House, Hartford, Connecticut.

of the cultural – especially the reading – environment into which Mark Twain married. It has evolved into the story of a courtship largely because the more I examined the similarities and dissimilarities between Samuel Clemens and Olivia Langdon, the more I wondered how they resolved their differences. As I studied 1860s Elmira and pieced together the Langdon family history I discovered an unexpectedly vibrant and intellectually engaged community and a family whose moral and social commitments suggested a very different profile from that which most of Twain's biographers had drawn, and I felt that this information was crucial to an understanding of the Clemens's relationship. With this, Samuel Clemens's own letters of the period reveal a figure who was more the settled bourgeois, the middle-class American who shared his contemporaries' basic assumptions, than I had expected him to be in 1868.

What interested me most was the – for want of a better word – "intellectual" environment of Langdon's and Clemens's courtship. For most of this century scholars have denigrated Langdon's tastes, values, and general education, portraying her as a neurotic nonentity in her youth and a paragon of dull propriety in her maturity. My own past work on nineteenth-century women readers had already taught me to be leery of blanket statements about female neurosis and ignorance, and I found that Langdon, like most of the other nineteenth-century American women who had the misfortune to come to the attention of twentieth-century critics, had been grossly caricatured by her husband's biographers. When I tried to look at Langdon's intellectual life I realized that she is most usefully seen within the context of serious nineteenth-century women readers – not the Margaret Fullers of the era, not the writers who read as an aspect of their profession, but the women who, never aspiring to authorship, read for information, for pleasure, for models, and for spiritual and intellectual improvement. Consumers of literature as of other tangible goods, serious women readers used books in their creation of a highly structured moral and material environment. In her life as in her reading Langdon strove to be a responsible member of this com-

8

munity, and her contemporaries were nearly unanimous in their praise.

Clearly Langdon's passion for books was one of her attractions for Clemens, as was his similar passion an attraction for her. Unlike their incomes and past experiences, books provided them with common ground. It also gave Clemens a chance to pose as Langdon's intellectual superior, an opportunity he eagerly seized and that has provided critics with ammunition for destroying Langdon's own credibility. But taking Clemens's airy superiority at face value effectively prevents appreciation first, of Langdon's own intellectual background and agenda; second, of the cultural values that she and Clemens shared; and third, of the respect with which Clemens often received her opinions. Their reading behaviors certainly reveal individual tastes and personalities, but they also demonstrate common cultural assumptions.

Until very recently, few critics have been willing to explore Langdon's life and values. The early years of the twentieth century saw a widespread reaction against the cultural assumptions that she represented, and nineteenth-century women, with the male artists (such as William Dean Howells) who supported them, became the victims of a generational rebellion. Olivia Langdon was one of these victims; in devaluing everything she valued, twentieth-century critics left themselves no way to evaluate *her*. Additionally in their need to paint her as a zealot of Victorian propriety they missed entirely her sense of humor, her flexibility, and her capacity for fun. It would seem impossible to write a biography of Mark Twain without knowing something of the mind, habits, values, and worldview of the woman with whom he lived for thirty-four years, but most of Twain's biographers have done precisely that, in the process skewing their presentations of their materials so that Clemens's family life is either ignored or misrepresented. Hence not just Langdon but also Clemens has been done an injustice. Mark Twain may have been as saintly or as devilish, as sane or as neurotic, as passive or as manipulative, as he has been painted by the various biographical camps that have tackled him, but he cannot be assessed without genuine attention to the people with whom he daily interacted – and the emphasis here must be on interaction, not mere reaction. Perhaps because it was composed of women, the family that most of Twain's early biographers portray is flat, a collective background for Mark Twain's angst and antics. And Langdon's own background is rarely more than suggested, and then only to be dismissed.

In the past few years scholars have attempted to address this issue, either focusing on Langdon exclusively or factoring a more complex character into discussions of Twain. In *Getting To Be Mark Twain*,[13] for instance, Jeffrey Steinbrink adds a rich and informed consciousness of Langdon and her Elmira connections to his study of Mark Twain's years in Buffalo. Reesa Willis has attempted a full-scale biography of Langdon in *Mark and Livy*,[14] and Laura Skandera-Trombley has explored Langdon's medical history, the women among whom she was reared, and Elmira's social history in *Mark Twain in the Company of Women*. Guy Cardwell's evaluations of Langdon in *The Man Who Was Mark Twain*[15] also attempt to resurrect something of the historical figure.

I hope that this book will contribute to Olivia Langdon's reevaluation. Inevitably, this entails shifting perspectives on the man she married. The more I began to know 1860s Elmira, Jervis and Olivia Lewis Langdon, and Olivia Langdon and her friends, the more I began to realize both how like and unlike them Clemens was. *Like*, in that they were all white Westerners, assuming in the depths of their being that their race, age, and culture were superior; like in that they all held (consciously at least) the same class values – the value of chastity, for instance, or of education, or of fiscal and moral responsibility. Like also in that they held the same assumptions about the material bases of good living, and that they agreed on the essential rightness of an ever-increasing horizon of activities, experiences, and expectations. They were *unlike*, however, in their modes of interpretation and their evaluations of cultural events, in their attitudes toward cultural authority, and in their faith in the reality of the word. They were also unlike in their rhetoric and in the paths, rhetorical and otherwise, that they took to achieve the goals they shared. Some of these differences were trivial, others profound. Some were the result of gender, others of personality, yet others of financial histories. Certainly the differences were sufficiently marked to make many observers wonder why Langdon and Clemens were attracted to one another. The answer given by early biographers – that Clemens wanted Langdon for her money and her status – has never been very satisfactory. More recently, some scholars have contended that he wanted her simultaneously to mother him and to represent the eternal virgin. No one seems to have wondered why *she* wanted *him.* Clearly, they were sufficiently unlike to merit the question. In the following pages I examine their dissimilarities and their similarities during the courtship period, and attempt to show some of the ways they negotiated their differences.

Chapter 1 of *The Courtship of Olivia Langdon and Mark Twain* examines Olivia Langdon's education and reading in its cultural context. Focusing almost exclusively on Langdon and her environment, Chapter 1 begins with an analysis of her commonplace book, contextualized through her family, particularly her mother, and through other women's reading in the middle of the nineteenth century. With Olivia's letters to her friend Alice Hooker and Alice's own letters to her mother, the commonplace book tells us what Langdon was reading during these early years and something of the ways she interpreted the works she read. Partly pursued to strengthen her inner self, and partly to familiarize her with her culture's most revered texts, her reading projects suggest how important written materials were to Langdon's emotional, social, and intellectual lives.

Chapter 2 begins developing the cultural ambience of Langdon and Clemens's courtship, focusing on Langdon's interests in science and introducing Clemens at the point of their greatest intellectual difference. Elmira in the 1860s was typical of many postbellum American towns in supporting several scientific institutions, including an academy of science, an observatory, and a serious science curriculum at the local baccalaureate institution, Elmira Female College. Elmira's intelligentsia, Langdon among them, were serious consumers of the rhetoric and methods of scientific practice as it was developing in midcentury America, and Samuel Clemens's responses to them demonstrate a radically different conception of modern science. His own sensibility valued cosmicity over positivism, and his scientific rhetoric was unabashedly poetic. Langdon's and Clemens's differing attitudes toward science highlight the difficulties of Clemens's courtship by showing the major intellectual challenges to his suit.

Chapter 3 focuses on Clemens's and Langdon's love letters, showing how they began overcoming their differences. This lover and his lady were actually separated during most of their courtship, while "Mark Twain" was on the lecture circuit, touring New England, the Middle Atlantic states, and the Midwest. Writing to Langdon every day – sometimes twice a day – Clemens launched a suit that has become famous in courtship history. Although few of Langdon's letters survive, almost all of Clemens's do, largely because Langdon dated and filed them as they came in. Only recently published in their entirety, and never before treated extensively, these letters demonstrate Twain's major rhetorical strategies for winning not only Langdon but also her parents. Whereas Chapters 1 and 2 begin portraying Langdon and Clemens's relationship by showing how different they were, Chapter 3 shows how they began to come together, largely through Clemens's exertions.

Chapter 4 juxtaposes Langdon and Clemens by examining them as readers – exploring their individual reading strategies, the books they read in common, and the similarities and differences in their responses to them, especially in their reading of *Dombey and Son* and *The Merchant of Venice*. It also picks up the discussion begun in Chapter 3 about the way they used books as courtship vehicles, a subject other scholars have discussed but – both because the full set of courtship letters was not available until recently and because earlier scholars did not take Langdon's own writing into account – that has never been fully examined. In this chapter, as in Chapter 3, I examine Langdon and Clemens's commonalities, especially the cultural values they shared, such as their joint anxieties over the issues of duty and control. Working with their records of their reading as well as with Twain's published writings (works such as "The Recent Carnival of Crime in Connecticut"), Chapter 4 shows how Langdon and Clemens struggled to control themselves, to control and thus familiarize new environments, and to control each other.

Chapter 5 moves from the courtship period to the early years of Langdon and Clemens's marriage, from early 1870 to May 1873, when they left for their first trip to England together. These brief years were chaotic, both physically and emotionally: few young couples experience the number of deaths and moves that Clemens and Langdon knew. However this crucible period also saw them growing together as a couple, staking out territories and developing the reciprocity that defines matrimonial possibilities. Chapter 5 especially examines Langdon's maturation, tracing her changing concepts of the relationships between herself and her God, her husband, her natal family and childhood friends, her children, and her new neighbors. It shows her continuing her education through the Buffalo and early Hartford years, and it demonstrates her evolution from a retiring young wife into a self-confident young hostess. By the end of this period, the relationship that had begun in passionate courtship had settled into a firm, often frustrating, and equally often joyous marriage. This final chapter traces the process through which Olivia Langdon and Samuel Clemens became Mrs. and Mr. Clemens.

1

A COMMONPLACE BOOK

We view the world with our own eyes, each of us; and we make
from within us the world we see. A weary heart gets no gladness
out of sunshine; a selfish man is skeptical about friendship, as a
man with no ear does not hear music.

Quoted from Thackeray's English Humorists in
Olivia Langdon's commonplace book

Between 1863 and 1871 Olivia Langdon kept a commonplace
book, a notebook into which she, and occasionally a friend, copied passages from published materials that she wanted to have
readily available – her own anthology of useful quotations. Like
other nineteenth-century commonplace books, Langdon's functioned not as a diary – a private arena for formulating and recording thoughts – but as a quasi-public document that linked
her, through the passages she chose to record, to her culture's
aesthetic, ideological, and intellectual discourses.

Although they do not function as arenas for creative thought,
commonplace books can tell us a great deal about their keepers:
about the transcribers' literary tastes, ages, genders, but most especially about their personal quests. The word "quest" seems
most appropriate here because commonplace books, as they functioned for nineteenth-century general readers, reveal the hopes,
fears, and longings of their keepers as much as and perhaps more
than most diaries. The commonplace book of a young woman

such as Olivia Langdon gives us insight, above all, into its keeper's vicarious explorations of life situations.

Though she was seriously ill between 1861 and 1864, most of the time Langdon kept her commonplace book she was not dealing directly with issues of life, death, or struggle. Rather, she was active and, according to her contemporaries, future-oriented. However, she was *preparing* herself to deal with life crises, and her book is one index to her search for frameworks that would aid and sustain her when these came.

One of these frameworks is a philosophy combining traditional piety and conventional femininity with what, in retrospect, is clearly self-creation in the Emersonian or Bushnellian strains. Several entries testify to her wish to be the kind of Christian who would accept God's will without protest, a strain of piety familiar to descendants of Calvinism. This aspect of her quest is most evident in the poem she titles "From the German of Julius Sterne," in which the refrain commands the speaker's heart to "hold still" despite the many trials God sends. Like Donne's "Batter My Heart, Three-Personed God," this poem constructs a reader seeking the grace of perfect submission to an often arbitrary deity. "He kindles for my profit purely, / Afflictions fiery, glowing brand!" runs the last stanza. "And all his heaviest blows are surely / Inflicted by a *master hand.* / So I say praying – As God wills! *And trusting on him – suffer still!*"[1] [sic]. Similarly, "The Changed Cross," a twenty-one stanza poem copied from a friend's commonplace book in 1866, records a Christian's struggle first to reject, then accept, the burdens she or he is asked to bear; the speaker moves from the refrained insistence that "My cross I cannot bear" to the final resolution that "henceforth my one desire shall be / That He who knows me best should choose for me / And so whatever His love sees good to send / I'll trust its [sic] best because He knows the end" (30–5).

This traditional piety also characterized the writing of Langdon's mother, Olivia Lewis Langdon (to whom I shall henceforth refer as Olivia Lewis in order to avoid confusion with her daughter). Between 1865 and 1866 Olivia Lewis kept a diary recording her thoughts and her own activities as well as those of her family, community, and nation. In addition to regular attendance at church and at Wednesday night prayer meetings, Olivia Lewis also dutifully notes her indebtedness to God: "This is the 33rd anniversary of my marriage," she wrote on July 23, 1865. "I would still record the mercy of the Lord." *"Livia went to church this morning for the first time in more than 5 years.* May my heart be filled with gratitude to my Heavenly Father for all his goodness to me and mine" (April 29, 1866). "This is Charlie's 17th birthday. May his heart with mine be lifted up with gratitude to God for his great mercy to us" (August 13, 1866). "The greatest boon I crave is that my household may entirely belong to Christ" (August 19, 1866). In turn, Olivia Lewis's piety was clearly a legacy from her own family: "Oh if I had a spirit of resignation to his will who is the sovereign Arbiter of all destinies how happy I should be," wrote Mary Ann Lewis, Olivia Lewis's half sister, in 1836.[2]

Prayer for submissive hearts notwithstanding, however, neither Lewis woman passively accepted her fate. Rather, both took the responsibility for their lives and spiritual welfare into their own hands. The context of Mary Ann Lewis's prayer is her dissatisfaction with the school in which she was teaching and her general discontentment with living at her father's house; shortly after writing this letter she left, apparently teaching her way west until she reached Oberlin, Ohio, in 1841. In the spring of 1866, when Olivia Lewis recorded a period of intense depression of both body and spirits, she began by praying: "My head still aches – *and my heart is heavy.* My Father in Heaven strengthen my weakness and show me the way" (March 25, 1866), but she also sought and found secular comfort: "March 29: At 4 this P.M. Miss Dickinson came to be our guest." "March 30: We are having a delightful chit-chat with Miss Dickinson, but my heart is worn and heavy." "March and April Lord's Day 31st: My heart was solaced by an earnest and intimate talk with Anna." The "Anna Dickinson" referred to here was the abolitionist and suffragist of that name; an intimate friend of Olivia Lewis and her family, she was an activist who believed that morality and regeneration come about

16

through active, not passive, agencies. Whatever she counseled Olivia Lewis seems to have been effective; the diary records no more laments.

Given her family's piety, it is not surprising that Olivia Langdon, especially as she emerged from four years of serious illness, should feel it her duty to learn to endure. But to accept God's trials did not mean to resign herself to passivity. Rather, it meant to prepare herself for life. During these years Langdon focused on educating herself morally, spiritually, and intellectually, a process that suggests both an ongoing pleasure in mental engagements and preparation for future activity. In addition to entries counseling submission and resignation, Langdon copied passages counseling activity and hope. In her commonplace book a quotation from Longfellow's "Hyperion" lies close to Sterne's poem. Isolated from its primary textual context, in Langdon's book the passage speaks directly to her, counseling her to "Look not mournfully into the Past," but rather to "improve the Present; it is thine – Go forth to meet the shadowy Future without fear, and with a brave and manly heart" (19).

As with many of the passages Langdon copied, here the reader the text originally constructs is male. As writers such as William Dean Howells repeatedly asserted, the multifaceted connotation of "manliness" in Victorian America included gentleness and piety as well as adventurousness and strength. When a woman appropriates a passage enjoining manliness, then, she may be selectively reading for those less aggressive male traits that she is assumed to share, such as gentleness. On the other hand, she may be reshaping the cultural definition of manliness as adventurousness and strength to give herself access to these qualities. In a culture defining women as peculiarly passive, passages constructing male readers, when taken over by female ones, suggest women who are actively creating self-images that stretch the definitions of the female. Moreover, although a commonplace book is not an original work, it is, for its keeper, a *reconstruction* of whatever she or he perceives as culturally or psychologically significant. As such, the finished product not only reflects a series of creative choices but also stands as an autonomous entity, designed to remind its keeper of her or his resolutions and ambitions.

In Olivia Langdon's commonplace book, passages originally addressed to men have special force, suggesting a reader intensely aware that she is at the very least able to control her personal ideology of life, and hence her reactions to events, if not the events themselves – a self-control that would sharply distinguish her from her husband. "Happy is the man who observes the heavenly and the terrestrial law in just proportion," runs a quotation from Thoreau. "Whose every faculty from the soles of his feet to the crown of his head, obeys the law of its kind, who neither stoops nor goes on tiptoe, but his is a balanced life acceptable to both man and to God" (29). "The Past belongs to Gratitude and Regret; the present to Contentment and Work; the Future to Hope and Trust" (90), counsels Henry Ward Beecher. And from Thackeray's *English Humorists*, the following: "We view the world with our own eyes, each of us; and we make from within us the world we see. A weary heart gets no gladness out of sunshine; a selfish man is skeptical about friendship, as a man with no ear does not hear music" (83). Echoing the nation's obsession with futurity, these brief homilies project readers eager to believe that they can and will master both themselves and their environments. For a young woman still suffering the effects of a stultifying disease, but also beginning to understand that a normal life may yet be possible for her, such passages inscribe a determination to maximize her own possibilities.

Prayers for a submissive heart and extracts espousing a cheerful optimism were not the only passages Langdon copied into her commonplace book, however. In tandem with passages prescribing self-generation she also copied those prescribing correct behavior for women. In doing so, she set herself up for potential role conflicts, for whereas homilies to self-generation encouraged open-ended exploration of self and world, most nineteenth-century advice directed specifically to women counseled them to channel their energies toward the circumscribed experience of wifehood and motherhood. Three passages directed to women stand out in Langdon's commonplace book. The first is a quotation from Martin Luther asserting that "a Woman is or at least should be a friendly, courteous, and merry companion in life, the honour and ornament of the house: inclined to tenderness – the pleasure, joy, and solace of her husband" (35). The quotation is followed by one of Langdon's rare commentaries: "Taken from Mrs. Brook's book of gleanings, a good description of herself."[3] The commonplace book also contains lengthy extracts from *The Merchant of Venice,* all of them Portia's speeches, and including the lines (often quoted in women's novels of the period) in which Portia describes herself as "an unlesson'd girl, unschooled, unpracticed" and declares herself happy "that her girlish spirit / Commits itself to yours to be directed / As from her lord, her governor, her King" (45–7). In addition, Langdon also copied a passage from a volume of Luise Mühlbach's *History of Frederick the Great* in which Frederick declares that the "vocation of making others happy, is the noblest calling for a woman" (57).

Like the passages celebrating submission, these all reflect a traditionally conservative view of women's nature and function, a view encouraging passivity rather than activity. Their appearance in Langdon's book suggests that in addition to searching for prescriptions for general human behavior, she was – like other women of her age and period – searching for prescriptions for specifically gendered behavior. The conflict latent in these very different sets of prescriptions marks Langdon as a member of a generation in transit between their mothers' religious piety and their daughters' – the New Woman's – social iconoclasm. In simultaneously accepting traditional feminine roles and appropriating male-oriented modes of being, women who came of age after the Civil War struggled to create new ways of being in and relating to their world. Certainly Olivia Langdon's early writings suggest that she valued traditional women's roles; both her letters, and reports of her by other people – in addition to the overwhelming evidence of Clemens's very dominating courtship letters to her – suggest that at least outwardly Langdon conformed happily and successfully to her culture's gender expectations. At the same time, however, the numerous passages urging self-creation in her commonplace book serve to undermine the implicit passivity of traditional women's roles just as they undermine the explicit piety of traditional spiritual roles. Seen collectively, these three groups of quotations construct a reader/transcriber who is struggling to create a self open to experience and change while remaining well within the culture's definition of femininity and Christianity.

Langdon's letters, as well as letters others wrote about her during this period, also reveal her piety, her traditional femininity, and her interest in self-creation. With this, they reveal her educational ambitions. Aside from the commonplace book, our best index to Langdon's character and interests during the years just prior to her marriage is the series of letters she wrote to Alice Hooker, a friend close to her own age, and the letters that Alice, while visiting the Langdons, wrote to her own mother, Isabella Hooker. The Langdons and the Hooker family had known each other at least since 1860, when Isabella Beecher Hooker, sister to Elmira's Congregationalist minister Thomas K. Beecher (and of course to Harriet Beecher Stowe, Catharine Beecher, Henry Ward Beecher, and the rest of the Beecher clan) visited the Gleasons' Water Cure and met Olivia Langdon, then at the onset of her long illness.[4] "I wrote so far, at Mr. Langdon's yesterday," Hooker wrote her husband John on July 16, 1860.

> I had a very pleasant Sunday of it – These friends are so really fond of me, for my own sake as well as for Tom's. . . . The only daughter, is my roommate for the present – Livy Langdon – She is a sweet young girl of Mary's age – but in very delicate health and I have helped persuade them to place her under Mrs. Gleason's care – She has been living on her nerves instead of her muscles all her life so far – and will not have *anything* left to live upon, pretty soon, unless she is made over.[5]

The friendship between Isabella and the Langdon seniors strengthened over the years, and their daughters, Olivia Langdon and Alice Hooker, also became close friends. After Langdon's recovery the two young women passed long visits in each others' homes in Hartford and Elmira and rendezvoused in New York for visits, where they shopped, visited museums and galleries, and attended concerts and plays.

Because so few of Langdon's own letters survive, Alice Hooker is probably our best informant about Olivia Langdon's personality, tastes, activities, and effect on others during this period, especially during the spring of 1867, when Hooker spent five months living at the Langdon mansion in Elmira. Hooker was a particularly lively young woman whose letters to her mother tell us much about the activities, culture, and relationships among the Langdons. Clearly awed by the family's wealth and fascinated by their cultural and social milieu, she was also Olivia's avid admirer. "You must think of me as settled in [the Langdon's] nice house," she wrote to Isabella Hooker on February 1, just after arriving in Elmira, "reading, studying, serving, sleigh riding, attending church arrangements, and going to parties, very happy and contented."[6] "Oh Mother what a nice thing it is to have plenty of money!" she added three weeks later. "They spend money very fast and freely here – and it is all very nice." And in the same letter she commented:

> You don't know how I enjoy being with Livy – she is so much more thoughtful, original, deep, than most girls and so is constantly making me go to the foundations of things. I feel very shallow sometimes by her but then am glad I am with her to get good from talking with her. Every night we read in the Bible and have a talk, one coming up very naturally and which started by what we've read gets off on to all matters of this life and the next. (February 24, 1867)

Bible reading, both as a solitary and a group activity, was common in the nineteenth century, and taken alone, Hooker and Langdon's evening sessions mark them only as particularly close friends. But as her commonplace book shows, Langdon's interest in religious matters extended beyond the Bible. With Hooker, she worked her way through Edward Young's *Night Thoughts*, an eighteenth-century poem epitomizing contemporary Christian views of mortality and immortality. "Openly hortatory," as a recent editor has noted,[7] this book-length, blank-verse poem's major theme was "man's mortality in the face of a divine judgement" (13). It also, however, stood as the most popular expression of the eighteenth century's faith in the mind's creative power (11), thus, for Olivia Langdon, speaking to her quests for spiritual rectitude and self-empowerment. Lines such as the following could easily take their place with other passages urging self-creation in Langdon's commonplace book: "No Man e'er found a happy life by Chance / Or yawned it into Being, with a Wish; / . . . An *Art* it is, and must be learnt; and learn't/ With unremitting effort, or be lost" ("Night Eighth," ls. 613–18). The poem appealed to both young women and became part of their regime of inspirational reading: "Livy and I are reading 'Young's Night Thoughts' . . . and enjoy them exceedingly," Hooker noted in her letter of February 24. She added:

> Some of the thoughts are very beautiful and plain, while some we have to study out, both looking over the book and writing our wits in the study. I never should have thought of reading them myself, but as Livy proposed it I did and am very glad of it now. There are so many quotations from it – every time we come across one we scream and exclaim "Is that from Young."

Although Young's popularity was fading rapidly by the 1860s, its past glories were inscribed in the frequency with which he was quoted in works written during the previous century. In reading and "studying out" Young's *Thoughts*, Hooker and Langdon were not only mulling over questions of immortality, as they thought, they were also learning how to recognize a primary way their culture sacralized and canonized literary texts.

Hooker and Langdon certainly did not spend all their time reading religious works. In fact, they played a good deal, going for rides and to parties (when Langdon was well enough) and spending hours, especially when the Langdon seniors were away, exchanging pranks with Langdon's younger brother Charlie and the other young men staying in the house. Still, although social events played a prominent role in their lives, Alice's letters to her mother highlight her and Livy's reading and formal studies more than any other ongoing event. Though consciousness of her audience may have partly dictated her choice of what to record – Isabella Hooker had once characterized Alice as "a fancy piece to amuse and please [rather] than a solid article,"[8] and it is possible that Hooker's emphasis on study was a strategy to change her mother's mind – and though her ebullience seems to undermine her dedication, still the amount of time she and Langdon spent on educational matters indicates that they did take them seriously. "Twice a week from eleven to twelve [we] recite to Prof. Ford, one of the college professors, who is a very fine man (young, unmarried too!) and who makes the hour of recitation most interesting," she told her mother.

> Livy and I are wild with delight over Philosophy and Prof. Ford's teaching – We enjoy it so much, for he comes to the house and we have cosy [sic] chatty lessons. After lessons, dinner and in the afternoon, we read History together, or rather are going to, but the book having been ordered and not yet come we have read Hawthorne. We are going to read French History. (February 8, 1867)

> We read Shakespeare together too – about half a dozen of the young ladies and Charlie meet Tuesday evenings here and each, having one or more characters, read some play. Livy reads very well and Charlie very finely. (February 24, 1867)

Darius R. Ford, professor of physical science, mathematics, and astronomy at Elmira College, had been hired to teach a private class in natural philosophy in the Langdon home; Hooker and Langdon's evenings may have been given to meditations on immortality, but their mornings were spent learning to measure critical mass. The Shakespeare reading group also found a place in Olivia Lewis's diary, where its rhythmic appearances suggest that it had become a local institution. On April 13, for instance, she noted, "The Young Ladies read Shake's Tempest this eve"; and on April 29, "Alice and Livia are reading French History, etc. This evening the house is brightened up by the coming in of the Shakespeare circle to read 'Much Ado About Nothing.'" Olivia Lewis's diary also records that her daughter had begun studying French language as well as French history, "Feb 12, Mary Nye gave Livia a French lesson this p.m."

Clearly, the course of study – or the several courses of study – Hooker and Langdon were pursuing were designed to equip them to understand at least the rudiments of their culture and its modes of investigation. It was not an education designed to radicalize their consciousness. Although scientific education itself was a relatively recent innovation, the texts Langdon and Hooker were reading, probably David A. Wells's *Natural Philosophy* and Julius Stockhardt's *Principles of Chemistry*, were not, in 1867, books that encouraged readers to challenge the status quo. Rather, with long-canonized works such as Shakespeare's plays, they upheld cultural values. The Shakespeare reading group, in addition to giving participants experience in dramatic reading and group analysis, also taught them (as did Young's *Night Thoughts)* the sources of well-known quotations and a series of famous plots. Read and discussed in a group setting, these texts would create readers secure in their possession of a significant aspect of their culture's wisdom. Touted as an aid to upward mobility – the image of the white working man who could quote the classics has always held a favored place in the stories democratic America likes to tell about itself – such an education could also be a conservative force, celebrating the authority of traditional works and communicating a general disapproval of the new. As we shall see, differing responses to the culture's traditional wisdom was one of the factors that marked Langdon and Clemens's relationship. That they were both familiar with the works, however, not only drew them together, but also meant that each felt sufficiently secure *within* the cultural canon to argue about it. Possession of the material – shared knowledge – provided the starting point for dialogue.

Just *how* secure any given individual would be in the presence of cultural wisdom depends, of course, on his or her prior background and anxiety level. For Hooker, the effects of Langdon and of their joint studies were, clearly, to make her examine herself and resolve to be better, especially in regard to her own character and intellectual development. Describing Langdon's vision of life as "sober and deeply thoughtful," Alice reflected that "she sobers me down somewhat . . . I did not know, before I left home that I had spirits any more cheerful or lively than every one else – but meeting as many people as I have, I have found that I am not cast down or cheerless as often as they are" (April 14, 1867). In addition to gaining insight into her own character, she also found that regular studying was improving her mind. Contemplating her return to Hartford, Alice vowed to carry her new habits with her:

> I do hope when I get home that I shant [*sic*] *waste* my time, read little and accomplish less – I am horror-struck with all I must know and which every school girl of seventeen does know – astronomy I pine to be familiar with and here at twenty know not a word of – ditto geology, chemistry, mental philosophy and other studies. . . . Anyway I know more French History than I did, which isn't saying much to be sure, and on several points I am a little better off than I used to be. (May 3, 1867)

Unlike Hooker, Langdon does not seem to have been overly anxious about the gaps in her education. However, even though she apparently did not discuss it much (at least in writing), it is clear that she continued to pursue determined educational goals. Langdon's letters, though not as articulate as Hooker's, suggest some of her reading and other intellectual endeavors. Apparently, Alice was not her only study companion. The group that came for Shakespeare readings – Alice and Clara Spaulding, sisters close to Langdon's age, and Emma Nye, another close friend – all seem to have participated in her study groups. "We [Langdon and Alice and Clara Spaulding] have finished 'Frederick the Great and his Court' it is extremely interesting – have you commenced it yet? We became very much excited over some portions of it," Langdon wrote Hooker in Hartford.[9] "Cousin Lizzie is still with me, we are now reading 'Aurora Leigh' together, perhaps you remember what a favorite it is of mine," she noted two weeks later (June 7, 1867). Apparently the Shakespeare group was sufficiently successful to expand over the next year, growing to include some of the older adults as well as Langdon's friends: "We read 'King Henry V' last evening" Langdon noted on October 30. "Last night Emma Sayles, Henry, John and Mr. Yates spent the evening here, this is the second meeting of our reading circle, since I returned," she continued early the next year. "We are now reading the 'Vicar of Wakefield' the boys have never read it." And in the same letter she says: "I am reading the last Vol. of the 'Rise of the Dutch Republic' and 'Nathalia' by Julia Kavanah [sic] – so you see that I am reading a novel, but keep that in my room and read it at night when I go to bed before Lottie & at such odd times. I do not bring it down stairs fearing that I shall spend too much time on it" (February 11, 1868).

This last remark is notable for what it tells us about Langdon's sense of the uses and pleasures of reading. Every other work either Langdon or Hooker mention is read either for information, inspiration, or moral education. Even *The Vicar of Wakefield* and Mühlbach's historical novels are clearly being received as didactic texts, not as fiction, for Langdon mentions *Nathalie*, not them, as "a novel." Of the genre long considered "women's literature," *Nathalie* was published in 1850 by the Irish novelist and essayist Julia Kavanagh and concerns the courtship of a passionate, independent protagonist by an older man, a courtship that ends in a companionate marriage. Although somewhat proleptic of Langdon's own romantic situation (she had met Clemens barely two months earlier), nevertheless it is clear, first, that Langdon ranked *Nathalie* lower on her scale of important books than most of her other reading, and second, that she was sufficiently compelled by the book to feel that she had to keep it out of temptation's way during the day. Both these attitudes are typical of women of Langdon's class and period: then as now, the

line between "educational" and "pleasurable" reading was fairly
sharply drawn, and though fiction was beginning to enter the
"educational" category, admissible texts – clearly *Frederick the
Great* and *The Vicar of Wakefield* fit the bill – had to be distin-
guished by some overtly moral, generally didactic, intent. "Serious and thoughtful," as Hooker described her, Langdon
occasionally read novels designed for pleasure during private
times, but clearly did not consider them appropriate vehicles for
her educational goals.

The profile of Langdon that develops from the records of her
reading and her studies for this period, and from the friends and
relatives who commented on her in relation to those activities,
suggests a young woman quietly determined to educate herself
according to her society's notions of what constituted culture and
literacy. Although gender was certainly a factor in her education,
it was probably less so in her case than in many others. Clearly,
the Langdon seniors encouraged her to pursue as high an education as she wished – they had enrolled her in the Elmira College preparatory branch before she became ill, and apparently
encouraged her to resume her studies after her recovery. They
were also comfortable with accomplished women, including public speaker Anna Dickinson; Rachel Gleason, who held an M.D.
from the Syracuse Medical College and, with her husband, operated the Elmira Water Cure;[10] Julia Beecher, Thomas K. Beecher's wife, who wore bloomers, bobbed her hair, and worked
closely with her husband; and Isabella Hooker, an open cam-
paigner for women's rights. And although the Langdons did send
their son to boarding school, when it became clear that he had
neither aptitude nor liking for schoolwork, they quietly placed
him in a business apprenticeship.

Class seems to have been far more important to Olivia Langdon's educational ambitions than gender. Although neither of
the Langdon seniors had much formal education (Jervis was
tending shop by midadolescence), and although they did not
achieve genuine wealth until their children were nearly grown
(their daughter Susan, in fact, was already married), they were

Langdon mansion, exterior, after renovations. Mark Twain Archives, Elmira College.

Langdon mansion, interior, parlor. Mark Twain Archives, Elmira College.

Langdon House, interior, study, late 1880s. The Mark Twain House, Hartford, Connecticut.

29

Group Photo at Niagara Falls, probably 1865 or 1866. Olivia and Jervis Langdon, first and second from right; their son Charles Langdon may be the young man seated in front. Mark Twain Archives, Elmira College.

Julia Beecher's Sunday School Class, *c.* 1855. Olivia Louise Langdon's picture is at the top; Julia Beecher is in the center. Mark Twain Archives, Elmira College.

Susan Crane, Olivia's sister.
Mark Twain Archives, Elmira
College.

Alice Hooker Day. Harriet
Beecher Stowe Center, Hartford, Connecticut.

clearly the type of middle-class Americans who read widely and who felt confident in their abilities to question, and at times defy, their society's "givens": the "given" of slavery, for instance, or of women's subordinate status – or, on a more personal level, the given that Samuel L. Clemens was an inappropriate choice for their daughter. At the same time, their *tastes* were solidly Victorian, in literature and music as in furniture and architecture. Genuinely interested in literature, especially fiction, Olivia Lewis and, one suspects, her husband, also used – consumed – literature as one element of their lives as middle-class Americans aspiring to (and achieving) the status that accrues with wealth. That their daughter Olivia also regarded book-learning as an adjunct to class is evident from a letter she wrote some years after her marriage, itemizing, with some annoyance, the obligations of a woman of her rank:

> I told Mr. Clemens the other day that in this day women must be everything. They must keep up with all the current literature, they must know all about art, they must help in one or two benevolent societies, they must be perfect mothers, they must be perfect housekeepers and graceful gracious hostesses, they must go and visit all the people in the town where they live, they must always be ready to receive their acquaintances, they must dress themselves and their children becomingly and above all they must make their homes charming and so on without end – then if they are not studying something their case is a hopeless one.[11]

To say that reading and learning were part of a consumer culture is not to claim that they could not also be agents of serious intellectual engagement to the consumers. Certainly Olivia Langdon seems to have borne a passion for education that other people noticed even though little in her own letters and diaries expresses it. Like Alice, Isabella Hooker noticed Langdon's consuming interest in books; unlike her daughter, she disapproved, claiming that so much reading contributed to Langdon's poor health. In her letters to Alice Hooker, Langdon constantly queries Hooker about her reading, her German lessons, and her painting.

While education was clearly a class issue, then, it was also a personal passion.

But even passions are culturally rooted. If we move from Langdon's immediate familial environment to that of her town and region, we see that her reading reflected her culture's educational values. Prominent citizens of Elmira had long publicly supported schools, libraries, and other educational institutions. In 1833, some of the local entrepreneurs established the Mechanic's Library, where, for two dollars a year (and free for apprentices), subscribers could borrow books for four weeks. Designed to serve the city's workers, the bylaws of the library specified that "no person shall be entitled to vote or to hold any office in said Library, unless he is a practical Mechanick."[12] Lodged in a building erected expressly for it in 1840, by 1853 the library contained fourteen hundred volumes. It was disbanded in 1863 after serving the community for thirty years.

A list of the library's holdings in 1843 suggests the kind of reading the library trustees considered appropriate for working men sufficiently motivated to subscribe. Histories (*History of New York*, Bancroft's *History of the United States*), compendia of useful knowledge (the *Encyclopedia Americana*), textbooks (Buffon's *Natural History*, Herschel's *Astronomy*), and the papers of eminent men (*Political Writings of Thomas Payne*) are by far the largest categories. Literature comes next, ranging from "Cooper's Novels complete" through "Goldsmith's Works," to "Shakespeare" and *Oliver Twist*.[13] The library also subscribed to a number of local (New York state) and national magazines and newspapers.

Possibly overlapping with the last years of the Mechanic's Library, and certainly picking up the slack after its demise, Beecher's Park Church also had a library. This, too, featured histories, biographies, science texts, and belles lettres, primarily, though not exclusively, from the Anglo-American tradition. Although many of the volumes in the earliest collection disappeared during the Civil War years,[14] approximately five hundred remain from the period when Langdon would have known the library.[15] These range from Carlyle's *French Revolution* and Giorgio Vasari's *Lives of the Most Eminent Painters, Sculptors, and Architects* to Taine's *History of English Literature,* Leckey's *History of the Rise and Influence of the Spirit of Rationalism,* and Darwin's *Descent of Man.* An 1870 edition of Herbert Spencer's *Principles of Biology* bearing Thomas K. Beecher's initials inside the front cover has marginal notations on paragraphs referring to adaptation and evolution. And an 1880 edition of *The Life and Letters of Horace Bushnell* was checked out by both Olivia Lewis Langdon and her daughter-in-law, Ida (Mrs. Charles) Langdon.

The collections in both libraries (which together served Elmira's cultural life for more than half a century) dictated an approach to reading that emphasized informational genres. Books of useful knowledge, and works on biological, physical, and chemical sciences, gave readers at least superficial access to the ideas, concepts, and *languages*[16] that were, in the mid-nineteenth century, rapidly becoming discourses of intellectual power in Western culture, while histories, biographies, and belles lettres incorporated debates that configured the past in terms of current interests and needs. All suggest readers grateful for the opportunity to add to their understanding of their culture's dominant ideas. Mid-nineteenth-century Elmira's libraries, sober and ambitious, implied a reading public that, from apprentices to business executives, sought to increase its access to, and ultimately its power over, the ways its culture conceived of its past, present, and future.

It was left to the booksellers to pander to less ambitious tastes. In the 1860s, two stores sold books: Preswick and Dudley's, which specialized in religious books (*The Blood of Jesus,* paper cover; *Child's Guide to Heaven, The Harvest Work of the Holy Spirit*[17]) in addition to recent novels, temperance tracts, sheet music, and other popular works; and Hall Brothers, which sold books, stationery, writing tables, board games, and wallpaper. Although either store could have served the Langdon household, the fact that "Fred Hall" was a frequent visitor there suggests that the family probably patronized Hall Brothers Books.[18] The shop's account books list *Aurora Leigh,* which Langdon mentions as a particular favorite, and "Kavanagh," presumably Julia Kavanagh's *Nathalie,* along with scores of other volumes ranging from contemporary fiction to histories, biographies, and works of travel and science.[19]

What, in the end, did all this mean? Very little questioning of a radical nature, one suspects, and often a very superficial approach. The *Advertiser*, the Elmira newspaper that, true to its name, tended to lavish praise indiscriminately, reported many public lectures that sound, even discounting the obligatory hype, as though they were designed more to render sensational than intellectual highs,[20] and the theatrical and musical performances – there were many – that came through town were designed for decidedly middlebrow tastes. Yet to say this is not to claim that postbellum Elmira was without cultural merit. On the contrary, one could argue that it was a cultural oasis in an area that had been frontier country within the memories of its older inhabitants. Most important, the kind of intellectual engagements the town's schools and libraries encouraged gave access to the cultural training that was an increasingly necessary part of upward mobility during the latter part of the century. To be familiar with the culture's canonized figures was (as women fighting for educational opportunities well knew) to at least symbolically partake of their wisdom; practically, to know Shakespeare and to quote Xenophon (preferably in Greek) demonstrated the requisite background for social approval and the avenues to intellectual power. Elmira's libraries, bookstores, and other institutions gave its citizens access to the languages and the debates of mainstream nineteenth-century culture.

Olivia Langdon's own education, then, was framed by her community's ambitions. With this intellectual environment, her physical surroundings, both on familial and community levels, and the striking mobility facilitated by a railroad culture, also affected the availability of information and entertainment. Not only was mid-nineteenth-century Elmira not a backwater town, the Langdon family were not provincials. First, Langdon's parents, especially Olivia Lewis, created a domestic environment that welcomed a continuous flow of friends, relatives, and official guests. Hard-working and clean-living, Olivia Lewis and Jervis Langdon had begun their married lives in 1832 as storekeepers, living in a series of small upstate towns until 1845, when they came to Elmira. By 1860 Jervis Langdon was among the richest men in town. Between 1862 and 1865, the Langdons bought the house and lands originally developed by the late Anson C. Ely, one of Elmira's most prominent citizens,[21] and in 1866 Olivia Lewis's diary records the beginnings of extensive (and expensive) renovations: "April 11, We took up the Library and recitation room carpets to make ready for the sliding doors." Renovations also included installation of a wash closet in the back hall, work on the attic, and a new kitchen: "May 11 The carpenters are cutting the kitchen loose to raise it up." "Wed 16th The kitchen was raised safely this afternoon and very glad am I that it is done at last." Apparently the Langdons did not find the kind of work they wanted among local craftsmen, so they sent to large cities for specialists: on May 11, "William Stymus came on from New York with his men to commence the Frescoing." On June 27 Olivia Lewis summed it all up:

> What a confusion we are in. The iron men from Baltimore are at work at the heating works in the cellar, the painters grainers and varnishers work is going on, the carpenters are in the kitchen, the masons are to begin their work, a man is polishing the piano, Ball and Black's man is at work in the drawing room and the white washers are at work in the chambers.

The result, apparently, was worth it all; the Langdon mansion on the corner of Church and Main became known as a site of hospitality, both for large receptions and for visitors staying overnight (For the night of August 29, Olivia Lewis recorded that "The number . . . lodged in the house was 27" [September 6, 1866]). Typical days saw a stream of family and friends. In Olivia Lewis's diary, these are noted in tandem with her record of Langdon's reassumption of her place in the community, suggesting that Olivia Lewis Langdon saw the family's social activities and her daughter's recovery as strands of the same social and emotional web. "Feb. 10 Fri [1865] This morning Livia breakfasted

37

with the family. The first time she has done so in three *years*. She also took dinner and tea with us. Doct. & Mrs. Merrell & Lizzie, John Greve, Hattie Langdon, & H. Eldred took dinner here. Mary Atwater & Kitty took tea." Later, the Langdons hosted large receptions, as when they entertained visitors to the State Teacher's Convention meeting in Elmira: "July 27, Thurs [1865] The number that came last evening to the reception was large, everyone seemed pleased. I invited Geo. Diven & his wife, Prof North (from Hamilton Coll.) & his wife Mr & Mrs Beecher & Doct Sayles here to tea. All went off pleasantly."

Visitors to the Langdon home remarked on its appointments, which included fine trees and greenhouses and, inside, not only the library but a conservatory onto which the dining room opened. This last most impressed Alice Hooker: "I do wish you could just drop in, take dinner here and feast your eyes while you dine on their beautiful conservatory," she wrote her mother on April 19, 1867.

> You know it opens out of the dining room, so as one sits at the table a vision of loveliness is before him or her. There is a lovely fountain in the center completely circled by the most beautiful flowers, heliotrope (how do you spell it!), roses, fuchias [*sic*] & azaleas and every other kind of sweet-scented and sweet-looking plant. Then besides the dropping and rippling of the water they have for music the songs of two mocking birds. It is a perfect little bit of paradise – the fountain flowers and birds flying around among them singing as only mocking birds do sing – and all this I have before me at every meal.

In addition to its familial warmth and hospitality, the Langdon home was also well connected to the larger society. The workers brought in by the Langdons to do the fine details of the house are one sign of Elmira's easy access to the rest of the country. Two hundred and fifty miles northwest of New York City and 150 miles southeast of Buffalo, the town has never been marked by its proximity to major metropolitan areas. In the 1860s, however, it *was* marked by the number of railroads that served it. One hundred forty-four railroads served New York state by 1869, many passing through Ithaca and Elmira and connecting with barges on Cayuga Lake and the Chemung Canal. John Arnot and A. S. Diven, prominent citizens of Elmira, were among the first directors of the Erie Railroad, managing it honestly and well until Daniel Drew, Jay Gould, and John Fisk destroyed it through their speculations.[22] Daily schedules for the Erie in 1869 connected Elmira with Buffalo, Cleveland, Dayton, and Cincinnati to the west, and with Philadelphia, Baltimore, and Washington, D.C., to the east. Additionally, the Northern Central served Baltimore, Philadelphia, and "all points South," as well as Buffalo, Niagara Falls, Rochester, Syracuse, "and all points East and West and the Canadas."[23]

This kind of service made the always peripatetic American even more eager to travel, resulting, as recorded in Olivia Lewis's diary, in days such as the following: "Jan. 24 [1865] John Ford came at 5. At 1/2 past 5 Miss Avery left for Baltimore, Sue for Lycoming and Lottie for Williamsport. Mr. and Mrs. Patten are preparing to leave in the morn." Later she wrote, "Was pleasantly surprised this morning on going out to breakfast to find Alice Langdon and little Nomie here, just in from Brooklyn. They left for Belimont on the 1/2 past 9 train" (February 8, 1867). Access to New York was apparently so easy that Jervis Langdon seemed, at times, to be commuting; Olivia Lewis's diary frequently mentions him leaving early in the week and returning on Fridays. The ease of travel facilitated Olivia Langdon's frequent medical sojourns in New York: "Oct. 11 [1866] Last night I suppose Olivia started for New York" (at this writing, Olivia Lewis herself is in Des Moines); and her triumphant returns home:

Jan 27 [1867] Lord's Day, This morning, we had a complete and joyous surprise. When we were seated at the breakfast table . . . Lottie & Lucius Stanley & Livia walked into the dining room. We could not have been more astonished & delighted. Theodore Sue & Dolly were the only ones of the family that had the knowledge of her coming. The plan of taking us by surprise was formed by Livia & Theodore some time ago. Lucius Stanley came with her & Theodore & Miki met her with the carriage at the Depot. The train was on time & she had a comfortable time & stood her ride well.

With the rest of her family, Olivia Langdon also used the trains to attend cultural events in New York. On November 28, 1867, she and Alice Hooker began planning a rendezvous in the city (the vacation that would see her introduced to Samuel Clemens): "I think that Father, Mother, Charlie and I shall, probably, go to New York within three weeks, and we shall stop at the St. Nicholas for two or three possibly four weeks, and we want you to be there with us . . . I think I should be able to do a good deal of sightseeing, you and Charlie would at any rate," Langdon wrote Hooker. A year later she recalls the visit: "A year ago tonight we went to hear 'Midsummer Night's Dream' – Do you remember?" (December 16, 1868). Friends and family members also traveled frequently: "Father will go to Chicago this month I expect," Langdon wrote Hooker June 7, 1868; on September 29, she reported, "Theodore and Sue had a most delightful trip to the White Mountains, Lake George and so on." Her mother's diary also records a long tourist jaunt to Montreal and New England in August of 1865.

This access meant that Elmira was connected to major cities in a very immediate way. People, goods, and cultural events flowed freely to and through the town. Elmira was a regular stop on various musical, theatrical, and lecture tours, and the local newspapers faithfully reported nearly all of them. The Y.M.C.A. lecture series, held during the winter months in Ely Hall, one of the town's main meeting sites prior to the erection of an Opera House late in 1867,[24] listed a typical schedule for that year. This included prosuffrage Theodore Tilton, editor of the Congregationalist paper *The Independent* (and eventually to be ruined by a scandal involving his wife and Henry Ward Beecher) with a talk entitled "American Women"; John B. Gough, speaking on temperance; George Vandenhoff giving dramatic readings from Bul-

wer and Scott; Benjamin Taylor reading his own poetry; and Anna
E. Dickinson, erstwhile abolitionist, suffragist, and defender of the
working class, with a lecture entitled "Breakers Ahead."[25] The
next year's lecturers included Louis Agassiz, D. R. Locke (Petro-
leum V. Nasby), Wendell Phillips, and Mark Twain.[26] The 1866–
9 seasons also saw performances of *Uncle Tom's Cabin* (*Elmira
Weekly Gazette,* June 9, 1865) and *Under the Gaslight* (*Advertiser,*
March 9, 1868), and by violinist Ole Bull (*Advertiser,* October 30,
1868, and *Saturday Evening Review,* April 17, 1969); actress Laura
Keene in *School, Hunted Down,* and *She Stoops to Conquer* (*Saturday
Evening Review,* March 20, 1869); actor Edwin Forrest in Bulwer's
Richelieu and *Othello* (*Saturday Evening Review,* November 11–12,
1860); and violinist Camilla Urso (Olivia Lewis Diary, July 21,
1865). Circuses, a Japanese juggling troupe, and many other popular plays and musical groups also appeared. Columns of the
short-lived *Saturday Evening Review* note cultural news on an
international basis: from the information that "Costat will not
conduct as usual, at Covent Garden," through the debate about
building a national gallery of art in New York City, to the gripping
news that "Victor Hugo has the largest head among living French
authors" (March 27, 1869, 5). Although much of this information went simply to satisfy (or create) a need for cultural gossip,
some, like our own worldwide weather reports for business travelers, served to alert peripatetic Elmirans to cultural possibilities
in the cities they were about to visit. The September 24, 1870
Saturday Evening Review noted that "quite a representation of Elmirans were present at Nilsson's first concert in New York, on
Monday evening" (8), another sign that townspeople moved easily between home and the metropolis for musical, dramatic, and
artistic events as well as business deals. Clearly, postbellum Elmira
was a crossroads where people, books, newspapers and magazines,
cultural events, and cultural information came together in a het-
eroglot mix that, although characterized by the high Victorian
seriousness of its most prominent families, also appealed to a pop-
ulace eager for fun as well as education.

Samuel Clemens was intimately involved in that peripatetic culture and, occasionally to his dismay, defined as part of its fun. During the courtship period, the trains that brought workmen, supplies, and entertainments in and out of the Elmira region also brought Mark Twain, who lectured through the Middle Atlantic states, New England, the Midwest, and California throughout the months that Clemens was conducting his furious courtship. His travels put him in a relationship to the Langdons that was at once familiar and threateningly alien – for both parties. For the Langdons, the relationship was familiar because Clemens was yet another of their many guests, arriving at odd hours and filling the house with life and companionship. They soon realized, however, that – as they themselves conceived and spoke of it – this guest was also a thief, intent on stealing their most precious possession. The Langdon seniors liked Sam Clemens and willingly extended their hospitality to him, but his visits also made them nervous. For Clemens, sojourns with the Langdons were like his visits with other families, such as his friends Charles and Mary Fairbanks in Cleveland; they were different, however, because his position as suitor heightened his awareness of the various disparities – financial, educational, and experiential – between him and the woman he sought to marry. The exigencies of his profession and the fact that he was always on the move, always dependent on the railroads to bring him to Langdon and to take him away, facilitated his courtship even as it exhausted and frustrated him.

During the years 1868–70, the time of Clemens and Langdon's courtship and engagement, Clemens sojourned in Washington, D.C., New York, Hartford, Elmira, and California. Beginning in the fall of 1868 and continuing almost to his wedding day, he lectured, in October, November, and December, first in Cleveland, Pittsburgh, and Elmira; then in New Jersey, New York, Pennsylvania, Michigan, Indiana, and Illinois. The winter of 1869 saw him in Ohio, Illinois, Michigan, Iowa, Wisconsin, Pennsylvania, and New Jersey. During the following fall he briefly established residence in Buffalo, where, with Jervis Langdon's aid, he had bought into the Buffalo *Express* and where he and Langdon planned to live. In November, largely to pay his debts, he resumed lecturing, covering Massachusetts, Rhode Island, Connecticut, New York, Washington, D.C., and Maine. January of 1870 saw him lecturing until the 21st. He and Langdon were married on February 2.[27]

This kind of traveling had its ups and downs. Always happy to play both sides of any fence, Clemens simultaneously deplored his lifestyle and exploited it in his letters to Langdon and others. Long days and nights on trains and dubious hotel accommodations (or, worse, restrictive hospitalities in private homes) were wearing, even on a comparatively young man of thirty-three. "I have now lectured thirty-five or forty times & am fagged out with travel," he told Frank Bliss on February 1, 1869 (*MTL* 3: 84). "I don't feel a bit well this morning, & so I cannot write," he told Langdon two weeks later.

> I left Ravenna about noon, Monday, for Alliance – lectured there that night – sat up till 2 in the morning (because no porter at hotel to call me,) & returned on a coal train to Ravenna – got to the Ravenna hotel just at 4 o'clock in the morning – went to bed for one hour & a half & then got up half asleep & started in the early train for this Titusville section of country – had to wait from 1 P.M. till 5, at Corry, Pa., & so I found an excellent hotel & went to bed – but several merchants of the place (I use the *nom de plume* on hotel registers when I am a stranger & want a choice room), saw my name on the register & called to see me (it was business, not idle curiosity – they wanted to get me to lecture,) & when they were gone I was feverish & restless & couldn't sleep. And at 5 I got up & soon started for this place, arriving just in fair time to open the lecture.

Clemens's youth, however, conquered all, here: "Good audience," he appended to the end of his woeful story, "& highly gratified with the lecture" (*MTL* 3: 103–4).

Such tours were genuinely exhausting, but they gave Clemens material for wooing. "And so *you* have been having visions of our future home, too, Livy?" he wrote Langdon on February 27.

I have such visions every day of my life, now. And they always take one favorite shape – peace, & quiet – rest, & seclusion from the rush & roar & discord of the world . . . it makes me ever so restive, Livy! – & impatient to throw off these wandering duties that thrall me now, & take you to my arms, never to miss your dear presence again. . . . How I dread the California trip. (*MTL* 3: 116–17)[28]

"I most cordially hate the lecture-field," he told his mother in a less poetic moment. "And, after all, I shudder to think I may never get out of it. In all conversations with Gough, & Anna Dickinson, Nasby, Oliver Wendell Holmes, Wendell Phillips & the other old stagers, I could not observe that *they* ever expected or hoped to get out of the business. *I* don't want to get wedded to it as they are" (*MTL* 3: 259–60).

For all his complaints, Clemens was fully aware of the compensations that accompanied his constant traveling. First and foremost, although he lamented the amount of time his job kept him away from Langdon, it also enabled him to come courting more often than if he had lived a sedentary life elsewhere. Additionally, that he was always a visitor in Elmira gave him the opportunity to actually live with the Langdons while he was in town. The household that was so accustomed to receiving travelers as they came and went across America became Clemens's waystation as it had been for so many others. Physical intimacy facilitated his acceptance into the family. From her initial fears about the stranger in their midst, for instance, Olivia Lewis progressed to warm affirmation: "I cannot tell you what a wealth we feel has been added to us, and radiated our family circle," she told their mutual friend, Mary Mason Fairbanks, on March 6, 1869 (*MTL* 3: 93, n5). Over the two years preceding his marriage Clemens began to regard the Langdons as family. At first, he was tentative; in November 1868 he surprised them at breakfast, poking his head through the door and announcing in what his biographer Albert Bigelow Paine described as a "low, humble voice," "The Calf has returned; may the prodigal have some breakfast?"[29] Knowing, surely, that the family was accustomed to arrivals on the early morning train dropping in for breakfast unannounced, he nevertheless clothed his intrusion in comic guise. Later, he was more confident. "Honey, I shall start home at 3 P.M. Friday," he wrote Langdon from Buffalo in late August 1869 (*MTL* 3: 323). By then, he had become a commuting fiancé, living in Buffalo during the week and spending Saturdays and Sundays in Elmira. The trains that took him away on lecture tours became, during this period, those that brought him home for the weekend.

Contemplative and very much a reader, Olivia Langdon grew out of an environment that, for all its wealth and comfort, was conscious of its own plebeian roots and committed to helping others. Physically frail, she compensated for her lack of mobility by traveling through the world of books available to her. Missing years of schooling because of her illness, she took courses to help fill the gaps. Surrounded by a family that defined itself in terms of hospitality, and by a town that earnestly combated the social upheavals of the postbellum period by establishing libraries, lecture series, continuing-education classes, and cultural events, she grew up in an environment of striving upward mobility. Like Samuel Clemens, she was an American who lived in an atmosphere of hard work and constant travel; like him, she was happy to engage in practical jokes with her friends, to party, and to go to concerts and plays. In many ways their similarities were more striking than their differences. Yet their differences also surfaced. These concerned both their educations and their interpretive processes, the fund of information they possessed and the way they evaluated it. Modern science, which in the mid-nineteenth century constituted one of the most exciting and rapidly developing public discourses, provides us with a way to examine some of the most radical differences between the cultural contexts of Olivia Langdon's and Samuel Clemens's educations and, most important, their individual interpretive modes.

"PHILOSOPHY & CHEMISTRY": SCIENCE STUDY IN 1860S ELMIRA

On March 12, 1869, the Elmira Academy of Science met at the Langdon home at the corner of Church and Main Streets. According to a newspaper account of the event, "about fifty Academicians and their invited guests"... were "elegantly entertained by their generous host and hostess."[1] In addition to ingesting coffee and cakes, the Langdon's guests listened to a series of papers on scientific matters, including a report by the outgoing president and new secretary, Francis Collingwood, titled "Recent Scientific Discoveries and Discussions."

Collingwood's overview touched on many subjects, among them new evidence concerning the distance of the sun from earth, the effects of tobacco on the human body, a recent polar expedition, astronomical discoveries, and new developments in the uses of metallic alloys. He devoted the largest portion of his talk to summarizing a lecture by Professor John Tyndall, of the British Association for the Advancement of Science, on scientists' tendency to take into consideration only "one set of phenomena, all going to prove a pet theory.... Whereas the *whole* truth is made up of *all* the phenomena from *all* sides of the question." The text of Collingwood's talk appeared in full in a report in the *Saturday Evening Review*, Elmira's short-lived "literary" newspaper, the next day.

Also on March 12, 1869, Samuel Clemens, then in Hartford looking after the publication of *The Innocents Abroad*, wrote to Langdon, by then his fiancée:

I remember that in a dream, last night, even *you* snubbed me in the most cruel way – but in my simplicity it seemed perfectly proper & right. I thought I arrived at the side gate in a carriage, & walked around to the front of the house, by the pathway, & as I neared the front door I saw you run toward the drawing-room window, making gestures with your hands which I took to be gestures of gladness & welcome – for I was expecting the same! But alas! they were to warn me not to enter yet, because the philosophy lesson was going on. I burst into the drawing-room door – but Mary stopped me & sent me to the library, & said you would come after a while. And as I went away I heard yours & professor Ford's voices discussing the properties of light, & heat, & bugs. But upon my word I was only disappointed – not hurt, not offended. Why do you treat people that way in dreams, I want to know? Why can't you behave yourself? (*MTL* 3: 162)

The immediate context of Clemens's letter – and doubtless his dream – is his report of a call made on Isabella and John Hooker at their Hartford home. Despite (or perhaps because of) their close friendship with the Langdons, they had made their disapproval of Clemens apparent. For him, the experience confirmed his reservations about calling on friends of friends: noting that "in former years I have been pointedly snubbed and slighted many & many a time," he claimed to have developed "a habit of *caution*" about paying calls (*MTL* 3: 162). The wider context of Clemens's dream, however, may have been his fusion of anxieties over his reception in both Hartford and Elmira. Like the mansion in which she lived, Langdon's "philosophy" lessons were a sign of her difference from Clemens, a difference in which he clearly felt himself to be the inferior party. He knew she was studying with Darius Ford, who also taught science at Elmira Female College; he may well have known that the Langdons were expecting the Academy of Science meeting at their home that night; he knew that, for all his travels and earned sophistication, Langdon had been more consistently exposed to formal – and traditional – education than he. Within that context, Clemens's dreaming that Langdon snubbed him while she was studying "philosophy" – that is, natural philosophy, the midcentury's term for physics – is not surprising.

But Clemens's aversion to science was not simply a matter of status anxiety. Its roots are philosophical and aesthetic as well. In *Mark Twain and Science: Adventures of a Mind,*[2] Sherwood Cummings has explored Clemens's attitudes toward science within the contexts of the fundamentalist Christianity of his youth, his deism, and his determinism. We can also explore Clemens's attitudes within a more immediate context: the spread of scientific practice and methodologies into the public sphere, and with that, the general acceptance, even valorization, of a scientific rhetoric that prided itself on its objectivity. Whereas twentieth-century historians have focused on the furor attending Darwin's works in the 1860s and 1870s – that is, on the debate between evolutionists and creationists – the fact is that other areas of science, especially chemistry, physics, and astronomy, were gaining widespread acceptance as authoritative ways of describing natural phenomena. For Clemens, the problem lay precisely with this methodological discourse: acutely attuned to the ways that language shapes worldviews, he felt that the language and methods of modern science signaled a thought process, including a set of basic assumptions, that radically falsified what he took to be "reality." In his courtship, his uneasiness with scientific discourse became a sign of one more difference between Langdon and himself; for in addition to its libraries and cultural events, Elmira prided itself on its participation in such discourses, and Olivia Langdon was an interested member of the scientifically inclined. This community – the citizens associated by mutual interests in scientific investigation – together with the kinds of texts produced by and for such a community, provide a case study of the rhetorical strategies developing in the field of nineteenth-century popular science. Most specifically, it sheds a new light on some of Samuel Clemens's discomforts about the intellectual differences between his fiancée and her friends and himself.

Langdon's Science Education

Olivia Lewis and Jervis Langdon clearly had wanted a basic background in science to be part of their daughter Olivia's education. Miss Thurston's Seminary, the Elmira school for girls that Langdon attended between 1850 and 1858,[3] stressed the study of science: the school catalog for 1851 claimed, "This Institution is designed to furnish young ladies with an opportunity to acquire a thorough scientific education, and at the same time to aid them in the formation of such a character as shall fit them for the active duties of life."[4] In addition to the Bible and liberal and fine arts, students in the junior class studied arithmetic, botany, physiology, astronomy, and natural philosophy; the middle class added algebra, chemistry, and geology; the senior class trigonometry, geometry, and logic. Mindful that "female education is often superficial, because much is attempted to be learned in little time," the principal urged parents "to permit their daughters to remain long enough at school, to obtain a thorough knowledge of the branches they profess to study." Langdon's parents, however, did not see fit to keep her at Miss Thurston's; although her sister Susan had graduated in 1853,[5] Olivia completed only the preparatory grades. At age thirteen, she entered the preparatory division of the college. Barbara Taylor suggests that Jervis Langdon's position as one of the founders of the college may have influenced the decision; at any rate, during the year Langdon spent in the preparatory division her courses were far less scientifically focused than they would have been had she stayed at Miss Thurston's.[6] Established because most young women were unprepared for baccalaureate work, the college's preparatory division offered arithmetic but no science as such; that seems to have been reserved for the actual college curriculum.

Langdon did not complete the college's preparatory division, either; confined by illness, she ended her formal education when she was about fifteen. Nevertheless the impetus her formal education gave her was lasting; she continued her studies the rest of her life.

Science was part of that continuation. Between 1867 and 1870, the years between her recovery from illness and her marriage, Langdon's letters to Alice Hooker tell us not only about her independent reading but also about her more formalized classes, including her studies in natural philosophy from Professor Ford. Just prior to the March 12 meeting of the Academy of Science at her parents' home, in fact, Langdon wrote Alice that "Professor Ford still makes me semi-weekly visits. I am soon going to take up Chemistry" (March 3, 1869). Apparently she was sufficiently serious about these classes to suggest to Clemens that Alice and Clara Spaulding, friends who shared her lessons, and Darius Ford come to live with them in Buffalo; on September 1, 1869, Clemens advised Langdon that "if we can get the Spauldingses & Prof Ford to live with us as you propose, we will keep house, by *all* means" (*MTL* 3: 325). Though serious language study preempted Langdon's limited study time after her marriage (the entire Clemens family became proficient in French and German), science remained an interest for her on intellectual, ethical, and pedagogical levels.[7]

It is clear that on some level these interests constituted a threat to the courting Clemens; it is also clear that he tried to gain the upper hand, at least on paper. Although his September 1, 1869, letter to Langdon suggests that he was receptive to her scientific friends, his dreams suggest that he also felt excluded from their circle. Earlier that year he had lampooned her lessons in physics and chemistry: "Livy and the Spaulding girls are taking Chemistry lessons & we are all afraid to stay in the house from 11 till noon because they are always cooking up some new-fangled gas or other & blowing everything endways with their experiments," he wrote to Susan Crane. He went on:

> It is dreadful to think of having a wife who will be always inventing new chemical horrors & experimenting on me with them. However, if Livy likes it, I shan't mind being shot through the roof occasionally & scattered around among the neighbors. I shall get rich on extra-hazardous accident-policies.

The family has got to be supported *some* way or other. (*MTL* 3: 181)

This letter is meant humorously and achieves its objective. Yet it, like his "dream," also suggests his discomfort with his fiancée's engagement in scientific study and experimentation, and shows us one of the strategies he developed to help him control the situation. Clemens's discomfort probably did not stem so much from having his wife know something he did not as from what Langdon's studies in experimental science represented of her investment in an enterprise about which he had serious misgivings. In this letter, as in all his writing, he seizes control of the situation by constructing an alternate reality, first caricaturing Langdon's studies, thus stripping them of the personal; then exploding them, substituting an image of violent destruction for one of disciplined investigation. In the process he also resolves his sense of exclusion by literally putting himself into the situation: in being "shot through the roof and scattered around among the neighbors" he moves from margin to center, from excluded other to focal victim. Nor does he rest until he has appropriated the entire scene: in getting "rich on extra-hazardous insurance" he caps his victory by becoming a con man – a manipulator not only of his insurance company, but of reality itself, for in this last move he makes himself the originator of the situation, the motivation for his wife's experiments. As in almost every document Clemens wrote about events and people that he encountered, here he reconstructs a particular community's reality to fit his own psychological and rhetorical ends.

But rather than continuing to caricature Langdon (a risky undertaking), Clemens preferred to woo her with his own version of scientific language, an alternate discourse that focused on cosmicity. Clemens's penchant for cosmic laws has often been noted; with cosmic imagery in general, they are the subject of many of his most vivid flights of prose. As Cummings has explained, cosmic laws and cosmic imagery were one sign of Clemens's struggle between the Calvinist/deistic/evangelical

Christian "strata" in his consciousness and the evidences of post-Darwinian science (16). But in addition to signaling an intellectual struggle, Clemens's cosmic imagery also signaled an aesthetic battle between a rhetoric that investigates the natural world according to an ever-narrowing strategy of containment – of strict, logical, deduction and induction – and a rhetoric that, like that of evangelical Christianity, permitted the construction and destruction of alternative "realities."

In his courtship, Clemens put this rhetoric to work to persuade Olivia Langdon that she should stay with him through "time and eternity." He also wedded this imagery to his most privileged theme, that is, exploration into the nature of loneliness and alienation. As his March 12, 1869 letter to Langdon admitted, by his mid-thirties Clemens had already felt a long history of slights and snubs; his courtship letters thematized his loneliness and figured Langdon as his redemption, whereas his later writings rehearsed, again and again, sagas of alienation. His language reflected his fusion of cosmic, philosophical, and domestic imagery, his alternative to positivism. Writing to Langdon about some recent articles on astronomy that stimulated his imagination, for instance, Clemens performed his own deductive process, taking star rays as his evidence and reasoning back from them to an imagined past – a past, not coincidentally, based in lives much like that which, he often told Langdon, would be theirs, once married:

> If we made a tour through space ourselves, might we not, in some remote era of the future, meet & greet the first lagging rays of stars that started on their weary visit to us a million years ago? – rays that are outcast & homeless now, their parent stars crumbled to nothingness & swept from the firmament five hundred thousand years after these journeying rays departed – stars whose peoples lived their little lives, & laughed & wept, hoped & feared, sinned & perished, bewildering ages since these vagrant twinklings went wandering through the solemn solitudes of space? (*MTL* 4: 11–14)

Presented in the language of passionate engagement and poetic wonder, Clemens's extended sentence performs the Whitmanesque function of sweeping all phenomena into its manifold images. Moreover, his description contains the antitheses that frame his courtship letters generally: in implicitly contrasting the "peoples [who] lived their little lives, & laughed & wept, hoped & feared, sinned & perished" to the "vagrant twinklings . . . wandering through the solemn solitudes of space," he refers to the many letters in which he tells Langdon that she will become the home, the center, for the "waif" he projects himself as being.[8] "Waifs" do not measure and calculate – at least not with numbers; rather, they seek solace. In using cosmic imagery to reinforce his courtship demands, Clemens is demonstrating his choice to use his power with language to deal in emotive, not "rational," discourse. Aware that the words he uses, the images he creates or manipulates, can "create" or "construct" the world he prefers, he goes for the persuasive over the rational, the imagistic over the mathematical, in the hopes that through it, he will convince others to participate in his vision.

In these ambitions he differed radically from most of his contemporaries. Although most biographers of Mark Twain have projected Clemens's difference from the family into which he married in terms of money, status, values, and power, Clemens's cosmicity – and his poetry – may be a sign of a more fundamental difference, that between believing and skeptical sensibilities, between positivists and poets. Langdon's scientific interests put her in the mainstream among her contemporaries; like them, she was interested in how things work, and willing to accept both current concepts of the physical universe and the specialized languages, or discourses, used to describe it. Equally interested in how things work, Clemens was not so ready to accept contemporary modes of investigation. Unlike most American liberals, he questioned the authority of scientific discourse. In the end, it was these languages, with their underlying assumptions and procedures, that fostered his skepticism.

Science in Mid-Nineteenth-Century America

Science in post-Civil War America was a heterogeneous field of emerging discourses and goals. On the one hand, the aura of elitism that was the legacy from the era of the gentleman scientist is discernible in the evolution of a scientific rhetoric that at once distanced the reporter of scientific materials from the phenomena he was describing and also reached for a vocabulary that would reflect the increasing complexity of the materials it described.[9] Additionally, the increasing emphasis on procedure (methodology) and deduction gave the discipline the tenor of authority granted in earlier periods to philosophy. The rhetorical homology between the study of Western philosophy and the study of Western science, in other words, brought to the new discipline the status and authority of the old, laying a groundwork for a counterdiscourse to theological readings of the natural world. On the other hand, many of the same men who were developing the new complexities of scientific rhetoric were also committed to developing a rudimentary grasp of scientific knowledge and procedures among the general public. In both cases, the *uses* of science were rarely presented apart from nationalist and imperialist goals. All of these trends are evident in a year-end report on the state of contemporary science written by a young physicist, John Trowbridge, and published in the *Annual of Scientific Discovery, or, Year-Book of Facts in Science and Art, for 1870.*[10]

Both thematically and rhetorically, Trowbridge's "Notes by the Editor, on the Progress of Science for the Year 1869" reveals the state and status of midcentury science. Making no clear distinction between applied and theoretical, "hard" and "soft" sciences, he treats, *seriatum*, engineering feats (the Pacific Railway; the Suez Canal), physics, chemistry, biology, social science ("the great problems of moral and physical evils incident to civilization," 179), astronomy, and geography. As much seventeenth-century religious poetry is structured around the language and ideology of contracts, so Trowbridge's report, especially as it refers to engineering feats accomplished in the United States, is structured by the language and ideology of commerce and exploitation. His introductory remark that the Pacific Railway opens "our territories to the enterprise of [both coasts] and to the cheap labor of Asia" (170) establishes the fact that the accomplishment is most valued for its contribution to capitalism; his subsequent remark that "electricity and steam are the great agents of civilization" (172) links capitalism with manifest destiny. Throughout, he associates technology and world power.

While his reports on technological accomplishments are structured to make these political connections, Trowbridge's reports on biological and chemical developments struggle to avoid prevailing arguments over the relationship between science and theology. Noting, for instance, that in biology "the theory of Darwin is steadily progressing in the estimation of naturalists," Trowbridge also reports that Owen's "derivative hypothesis," that living beings develop from inanimate matter, has also become popular (178). At the same time, he quotes chemist Jean-Baptist Andre Dumas's confession that chemistry is still "ignorant of the mode of generation" (177). Finally, Trowbridge writes his report largely in the passive mode, distancing his characters (other scientists) from their subjects and himself from his entire project. As a verbal construct, his document stands, seemingly self-generated and hence impersonal, authoritative.

Trowbridge's report, then, reflects the state of science and technology in 1869; that is, its explicit association of technology and capitalism, its studious avoidance of discussions of first causes, and its rhetorical frameworks, which were already projecting all scientific endeavors as "objective," as the methodological oracles, stripped of personality or ideology, that reveal natural law.

Both these rhetorical frameworks and the national interest in science are evident in the period's popular press as well as in scientific reports. Newspapers and magazines initiated columns reporting scientific news, teaching rudimentary scientific facts and explaining scientific phenomena. Additionally, publications devoted exclusively to science proliferated – for instance, *Scientific American,* which began publication as a weekly newspaper in

1845,[11] and *Popular Science Monthly,* started in 1872, as well as more specialized journals such as *American Naturalist,* begun in 1867. Like Trowbridge's report, many of these journals defined "science" broadly: articles in the first few issues of *Popular Science Monthly,* for instance, ranged from Spencer's series, "The Study of Sociology," through a report on an eclipse, a study of the causes of dyspepsia, an intricate article titled "Sight and the Visual Organ," to an argument about women and political power.[12] Even the professionally oriented *American Journal of Science* cast a wide net: in 1868 articles ranged from a "Sketch of a Journey from Canton to Hankow, through China," to Tyndall's evaluation of Faraday's discoveries.[13]

Then as now, most of these journals were written for popular consumption; the *American Journal of Science,* known popularly as "Silliman's," after its editor, Benjamin Silliman, Sr., was the only regular publication aimed at a professional class. The proliferation of popular magazines was one sign that science writers saw the lay readership as scientifically educable. "The *Popular Science Monthly* will make its appeal not to the illiterate, but to the generally-educated classes," notes the introductory column of that magazine's "Editor's Table" in 1872.

> The universities, colleges, academies, and high-schools of this country are numbered by hundreds, and their graduates by hundreds of thousands. Their culture is generally literary, with but a small portion of elementary science; but they are active-minded, and competent to follow connected thought in untechnical English, even if it be sometimes a little close. Our pages will be adapted to the wants of these, and will enable them to carry on the work of self-instruction in science.[14]

In its self-appointed task of "diffusing" science,[15] *Popular Science Monthly* was helped by the schools, especially the colleges and universities, which, from at least the 1840s, began adding courses in theoretical and practical science to their curricula. Elmira, by then a well-established town in New York state's southern tier, was similar to many American towns in its evolving interest in teaching science on both the high school and college levels. The 1840 catalog of the Elmira Academy, a private high school established in 1836, lists astronomy, chemistry, physical geography, natural history, natural philosophy, and trigonometry among its many offerings,[16] whereas the Elmira Female College required semesters of algebra, physical geography, botany and zoology, geometry, natural philosophy, chemistry, "conic sections and astronomy," "descriptive astronomy, with use of instruments," and geology and mineralogy.[17]

Textbooks, too, strove to make basic science facts and methodologies accessible to the general public as well as to students formally enrolled in courses. In keeping with the international nature of science study, many of these originated in Europe. Dr. Julius Adolph Stockhardt's *Principles of Chemistry, Illustrated by Simple Experiments*, for instance, had by 1859, the year it was translated into English, gone through at least five German editions.[18] This text, with the text on natural philosophy mentioned later in this section, were used in Elmira College chemistry and physics classes in the 1860s. They were also probably the ones Langdon and her friends used in their science classes at the Langdon house.[19] The experimental apparatus they recommended was cheap and accessible, and they were clearly written. Overall, they were successfully designed for students working at home as well as those taking formal classes.[20]

By the year 1869, then, science study, in the United States as in Great Britain and Europe, was a rapidly growing industry, one viewed not only as the province of an elite group of highly trained men, but also as a field of possibility for the general public, including women. The endeavor, seen as international, seems to have been moving in two directions. First, the trained scientists, men such as Trowbridge, supported by journals such as the *American Journal of Science*, were striving not only for specific knowledge but for a distanced rhetoric that, invested with the authority of mystery, would help them gain status in the (still liberal-arts oriented) universities. Pioneers, these scientists were seeking to institutionalize a field that, prior to the nineteenth century, had

Elmira College Observatory, 1863. Mark Twain Archives, Elmira College.

(*opposite, top*) Transit Telescope, Elmira College Observatory. Mark Twain Archives, Elmira College.
(*opposite, bottom*) Darius Ford, Professor of Science at Elmira College. Mark Twain Archives, Elmira College.

59

always been the province of a private elite. At the same time, however, interested practitioners were also eager to "diffuse" scientific skills and methodologies throughout the general public. Local scientific societies, a legacy from the days of the gentleman scientist, were, like the journals that sought to serve the general clamor for scientific education, part of this (ironically now democratic) direction. Both Langdon's studies in science and the records of Elmira's science institutions reflect this national mission, suggesting another arena in which this upstate town was connected to contemporary intellectual events.

Science in Elmira

In *The Launching of American Modern Science, 1846–1876*, Robert V. Bruce traces the development of local scientific societies, locating the most influential and well-endowed in the areas of New England and the mid-Atlantic states, but also showing their struggle to exist in the South and the Midwest. The most successful were, not surprisingly, affiliated with institutions that could lend facilities, prestige, and cash; these, in turn, tended to be located in large cities with histories of intellectual zeal, such as Boston and Philadelphia (35).

Although they could nurture budding scientists, one of the dangers inherent in local scientific societies was the high proportion of amateurism among their members, a legacy from the days of the gentleman scientist. Many, as a contemporary described them, were composed of "gentlemen who . . . are 'friendly to science' and its cultivation. Many of them pursue science only as a recreation during leisure hours, some are pleased to observe and know what others do, and others are content to encourage those who work."[21]

Elmira's local society, the Academy of Sciences, seems to have been fortunate in this respect: largely because of the existence of Elmira College, the members of the academy were in all likelihood a notch above the majority of similar local societies. Of its first five trustees, one, Charles Samuel Farrar, had a reputation as a scientist and a teacher of science that was known beyond Elmira. Clearly in a commanding position in the field of scientific education, he had already designed an astronomical observatory for the town and a thousand-pound globe for the students of the college; he would later be bought by Vassar at more than twice his Elmira College salary.[22] Another trustee, Thomas K. Beecher, professionally the minister of the Independent Congregationalist [Park] Church, was also a sophisticated amateur scientist and inventor. Francis Collingwood, academy president from 1867–9 and then its secretary, is listed in the 1869 Elmira directory as a civil engineer and a surveyor; the *Elmira Daily Advertiser* refers to him as the "City Engineer."[23] Several of the officers and committee members listed for the year 1860 were medical doctors, and Darius Ford, a member of the academy and later director of the observatory, is listed in the September 1869 Elmira College bulletin as the "Reverend D. R. Ford, A.M., Professor of Physical Science, Mathematics, Astronomy." With both master's and doctoral degrees in divinity from Brown University, he was, like Thomas K. Beecher, also well-trained in science; according to Gilbert Meltzer he appreciated Darwin's work and was especially interested in the relationship between geology, paleontology, and human development. The rest of the trustees, officers, and committee members were businessmen, lawyers, or judges.

Callisophia, a literary magazine written by the women of the college, ran periodic reports on meetings of the Academy of Science that tell us about the subjects members investigated and the general tenor of their debates. Women seem to have participated in the academy as members if not as active debaters; the 1897 reprint and update of the Academy's charter lists Dr. Adelle Gleason, Mary P. Joslyn, and Harriet A. Rathbone as fellows,[24] and the fact that *Callisophia* reported on the meeting indicates that women were not excluded from attending. The debates followed a set pattern. Generally, selected participants would be assigned the job of researching a given subject, to be discussed at a subsequent meeting. The meeting for October 8, 1860, for instance, which was conducted by Drs. Murdoch and Gregg, with Mr. Collingwood and the Reverend Mr. Bement participating, debated whether the "change of the shore water mark on the Gulf of Mexico" was caused by the land rising or the water level lowering.[25] Those presenting information had to be sufficiently prepared to field questions from other, possibly as knowledgeable, members: in this session, the chair argued for sedimental buildup of the shoreline, whereas another member suggested that "these elevations [are] sometimes caused by sudden upheavings." As in Trowbridge's report, at least some members associated science and imperialism; hearing that Bement believed that Florida once extended to Cuba and South America, Judge Brooks remarked, "If this be true, it would be a good reason, politically, for the annexation of Cuba." Echoing the substance and the forms of the national fascination with scientific developments, the academy clearly was a locus for discussion and dissemination of scientific information.

In addition to the academy, Elmira boasted an observatory holding a telescope, an "Equatorial Refractor of 8 1/2 in. aperture, with clock-work adjustments," as well as a transit telescope and chronometer.[26] The observatory had been established near the grounds of Elmira College in 1860; by the 1870s it also possessed a sidereal clock, a chronograph, and a scientific library and museum. Owned by the academy, the observatory was available for the instruction of the town: it enabled the college to offer (for an extra fee) classes in astronomy to its students; it let members of the academy practice astronomy as well as read the literature, and it allowed townspeople to attend occasional lectures and demonstrations. Olivia Lewis's diary, for instance, records that on April 26, 1867 "Theodore [husband to her daughter Susan], Sue, Alice [Hooker] and Charlie [her son] went up to the observatory at the College and had a fine look at the stars." Documents of the period that mention the observatory do so with a good deal of pride; in fact, the observatory was equipped with the instruments to make fairly accurate astronomical observations.[27] With this basic equipment, the presence of academy members with experience in astronomical calculations and observations, and a modest library, the observatory could serve as a major educational institution in the town.

Collingwood's overview of scientific developments began by claiming that "the present age, more than any other . . . is one of close study and observation" and clearly members of the scientifically interested community in Elmira in 1869 saw themselves as part of an international project to observe, measure, classify, and otherwise rationalize the study of natural phenomena. In tandem with this taxonomic project they bureaucratized themselves: the academy had a chair, officers, and trustees in addition to a membership; it assigned questions to members to be researched and reported on at subsequent meetings, and it valued searches of existing literature as part of its order of procedure. The town's scientific establishment not only employed material tools, then, it also carefully *contained* its methodology and its personnel: by bureaucratizing and hierarchizing its adepts and insisting upon a careful procedure for its experiments and data collections. Like its counterparts throughout the country, Elmira's scientific establishment contained and controlled data and their interpretation.

Mark Twain and Science

This routinization, on both a rhetorical and a bureaucratic level, was part and parcel of the development of modern science. Devoted to methodological order, it was not open to protest against the logic that framed its conclusions. And there, for Mark Twain, was the rub. Never afraid to challenge philosophical assumptions, Twain was skeptical of methodological claims to truth. Much of his attack on science was in fact an attack on methodologies, especially deduction, which, as a method for arranging information and solving problems, was the target of many of his best deconstructive satires. Rather than theology being the basis for his suspicion of certain sciences, as Cummings claims (27), shoddy thinking and rigid rhetoric may have been his real objection. A short piece published in 1871, shortly after he was married, illustrates these concerns, showing how Twain's humor often masked probing questions about scientific assumptions.[28]

In "A Brace of Brief Lectures on Science" Twain explicitly links scientific and police processes, comparing the deductive reasoning of paleontologists with the apparently fruitless detective work being conducted in the case of Benjamin Nathan, a stockbroker who had recently been murdered in New York City. Beginning with the implication that the police investigating the case are incompetent because they have been unable to draw any conclusions from the evidence at the site of the crime, Twain segues into his critique of paleontologists by suggesting that "one deep paleontologist" could do the work of twenty detectives:

> Let me demonstrate that with no other clue than one small splinter off that "iron dog," or a gill of the water the bloody shirt was washed in, any cultivated paleontologist would have walked right off and fetched you that murderer with as unerring certainty as he would take a fragment of an unknown bone and build you the animal it used to belong to, and tell you which end his tail was on and what he preferred for dinner.[29]

The object of "A Brace of Lectures" was to prove that science is reductive, first, because it builds grand theories on scanty evidence, and second, because in seeking to reason "objectively," scientists omit commonsense – and by that Twain meant the evidence of contemporary experience – from their reasoning process. On the topic of why bones found in primeval sites are broken lengthwise, for instance, Twain attacks the paleontologists' claim that it was for the extraction of marrow by arguing,

> Why should [Primeval Man] break bones lengthwise to get at the marrow when anybody except a scientist knows that it is a deal easier to break a bone crosswise than lengthwise, and still more convenient to smash your stone down on it and let it break any way it pleases; and we all know that the marrow will taste just the same, no matter what plan of fracture you pursue. And yet nothing would suit this primeval "galoot" but the lengthwise style – it does *not* look reasonable. (534)

And "reasonable," Twain claims, is a hallmark of primitive man, if not of his descendants: "I have always noticed that your Primeval Man looks to convenience *first*" (534).

In the end, what disturbs Twain is the claim to proof, both in cases of inadequate evidence and in light of the fact that every theory thus created is eventually destroyed. Assuming, briefly, the guise of the scientist, his narrator remarks, "If any one ... should say ... that in establishing one paleontological position ... I generally demolish another, I would answer that these things are inseparable from scientific investigation. We all do it – all scientists" (537). And he lays the source of the problem to the nature of science itself: "Science cannot help it. Science is full of change. Science is progressive and eternal" (538). Rather than a change of tone, a final obeisance to science, as Cummings and Hill see it, this last paragraph continues Twain's attack on science's claim to certainty amid its continual contradictions and reversals.[30]

The ubiquitousness of these claims were evident in almost any publication of the period, including those in which Twain published his own work. As Sherwood Cummings notes, Clemens's substantial publications on science begin about 1870, when he and Langdon, newly married, were living in Buffalo. There, in addition to his duties on the *Buffalo Express*, Clemens also wrote for the *Galaxy*. Like many newspapers and magazines of the period (including the Elmira *Advertiser*), the *Galaxy* ran a column entitled "Scientific Miscellany," reporting and explaining scientific news. In 1874, the column featured an article by Charles Boysett on "Science and the Moral Order," in which the scientific method was defined as "collect[ing] facts eagerly, steadily ... Then, from these facts patiently observed, brought together, coordinated, classified, science deduces a *law*, a positive law, which is the expression of reality, of truth itself."[31] Cummings uses this quotation as part of his argument that Clemens, with others of his time, valued the idea of a natural order and was troubled, as well as exhilarated, by the discoveries of contemporary science. With this, it may also be useful to examine Boysett's ideas through

Clemens's ambivalence about the scientific method. Boysett's definition of the scientific method divides into two parts: a description of the method of gathering data and a description of what scientists do with it. As with any written document, readers, according to their personal and cultural perceptions, can emphasize either part. Clearly, for the members of a community interested in scientific developments, observation and classification would be perceived as equally important as deduction, and deduction itself would be a tentative process, beginning as hypothesis and progressing perhaps to theory, but not to the finality of "positive law."

Clemens, on the other hand, would be most likely to emphasize the latter part of Boysett's statement; for him its significance would lie in the idea that law is the end of scientific investigation, and that it represents reality, "truth itself." Seen through Clemens's eyes, Boysett's assumptions are suspicious. Boysett does not imply that scientists' conclusions might be tentative; he does not, for instance, use the words "hypothesis" or "theory." Rather, he suggests that scientists "deduce" laws, much as hens, given the right ingredients, create eggs. Read through Clemens's concerns, Boysett's conclusion is worded to contribute to Clemens's frustration over the rhetorical limits of deductive and inductive methodologies.

With this, Clemens was acutely aware of the potential (indeed, during this period the likelihood) that science's discoveries would be appropriated by groups more interested in exploitation than in research – such as the academy member who suggested the annexation of Cuba. Himself an expert in the rhetorical construction of realities, Clemens sensed that the authority of scientific discourse might be played for power ends. In "Science vs. Luck," written in 1870, he uses a lawyer – whose rhetorical gestures he equates with sham – to negotiate a differentiation between games of chance, which were illegal, and games of science, which were not. In formulating an "experiment" to prove his case – setting the two halves of the jury to play "seven-up" against one another to determine whether the "luck" side or the "science" side won, and arranging the teams so that the expert card sharks are all on the "science" team, the lawyer proves his case that "seven-up" is a game of science. "That is the way that seven-up came to be set apart and particularized in the statute books of Kentucky as being a game not of chance but of science, and therefore not punishable under the law," the story ends.[32] Science, we are subtly reminded, is not subject to civil or criminal law; it is, rather, a law unto itself. The clever con who can appropriate its authority can play the rest of society with impunity.

"Science vs. Luck" is a comic sketch in the tradition of southern and southwestern humorists of a generation earlier. Unlike "A Brace of Lectures on Science," it does not present itself as a commentary on scientific methodologies (although it could be seen as a comic myth, a study of origins). Nevertheless it conveys Twain's consciousness that scientific discourse, like legal discourse, may well be just another form of rhetorical power.

"Some Learned Fables for Good Old Boys and Girls," published in 1874, foregrounds these concerns. This first of Twain's attempts to satirize androcentrism by shifting the site of subjectivity (here, to bugs) and the definition of micro- and macrocosms (the bugs study "fossil" evidences of human life; a railroad track is taken to be the vernal equinox; a train to be the transit of Venus) in many ways catalogs his grievances with the scientific world. Additionally, its narrative point of view anticipates later Twain narrators, such as that of *Joan of Arc*, who speak simultaneously from inside a community of naifs and from a sufficient distance to analyze, if not satirize, that community. Beginning as a Kiplingesque fable ("Once the creatures of the forest held a great convention"),[33] about halfway through the first part (in a scene detailing a drunken orgy), the narrator reveals himself to be a member of the expedition, and he continues his story in the first person plural. From this vantage point, he reconstructs the expedition's hierarchy, from the august scientists ("Professors") that head it, through the "Spiders to carry the surveying chain and do other engineering duty," to the "Ants and Tumble-Bugs to fetch and carry and delve" (612). Most particularly, he creates the Tumble-Bug, the lowliest and most despised member of the company who is, not surprisingly, also its truth teller.

In addition to attacking scientists' self-aggrandizement and abuse of their positions as intellectual adepts (the plain-speaking Tumble-Bug is constantly denigrated by his superiors) "Some Learned Fables" also reiterates several of the themes Twain had satirized in his earlier pieces on science, especially paleontologists' arrogant tendency to reconstruct species from fragmentary evidence, and all scientists' unquestioning acceptance of positivism as a method for determining truth. Foremost among his themes is a burlesque of scientific language, from the nonsense of Professor Snail's reports ("The result of my perlustration and perscontation of this isoperimetrical protuberance is a belief that it is one of those rare and wonderful creations left by the Mound Builders" [628]) to the naming of new discoveries after their discoverers and then translating the names into dead languages (615 and 619). Additionally, Twain devotes a fair proportion of "Fable" to satirizing scholars' methods for deciphering unknown languages (623) and their tendency to find that ancient inscriptions confirm their own cultural myths (627). There are, moreover, a few hints that Twain associated some of his scientific nonsense with the Elmira scientific community – one "ancient inscription" found by the expedition refers, scornfully, to "these sleapy old syentiffic grannys from the Coledge" (626), whereas the reference to the transit of Venus suggests that Clemens had visited the observatory and listened to discussions about how to use its transit telescope to track the planet's path. If Twain did associate these with Elmira, it was only because Elmira's scientific community fit into Clemens's a priori onus against science – its language, its methods, and its hegemonic intentions. Clemens sensed that in their quest for "objectivity," scientific practitioners were oblivious to the degree of subjectivity, self-interest, and power seeking they had invested in their work.

Law – any law – tended to be a red flag to Clemens. One of the targets of his later anger was the existence of scientific or natural laws, in part because of the way they could be used to justify human power plays, but mostly because he hated to admit how much they controlled him. This may mark the point of his greatest intellectual and aesthetic distance from Olivia Langdon and her circle. Whereas they weighed and measured, contentedly uncovering the rules governing the world, Clemens identified with the free spirits that roamed with "no limits of any kind."[34] For him, then, modern science was restrictive and personally repugnant, and he sought an alternative discourse that would circumvent the rigidity of scientific laws. Whereas the Elmira community was interested in science as description, classification, and hypothesis, that is, as rational discourse, Clemens was attracted to it as cosmic magic, and he preferred to treat cosmology as rhetorical eschatology. Entry into the Elmira community, then, represented for Clemens a close association with people whose intellectual outlook would be, for him, disturbingly methodological.

For all these reasons, Clemens had cause to be leery of the investments in scientific discourse of his fiancée, her family, and her community. Nevertheless, his doubts about their intellectual preferences did not deter his own project among them. Clemens's dream that Livy snubbed him during a physics lesson existed in tandem with his fantasy that he could turn her science studies to his own advantage. For all his skepticism about scientists' hegemonic intentions, he had a few of his own. Dominant among them was his intention to marry Langdon, no matter how many differences of intellect or class lay between them. In the plan he evolved to carry out this project, cosmic imagery became not so much an alternative to positivist language as a rhetorical trope for making love. Setting aside his role as skeptic and assuming his role as arch manipulator of discursive modes, Clemens drew on all of his literary experiences to negotiate his way into the Langdon family.

3

NEGOTIATING DIFFERENCES: LOVE LETTERS AND LOVE TEXTS

The most degraded sinner is accepted and made clean on high when his repentance is sincere – his *past* life is forgiven & forgotten – & men should not pursue a less magnanimous course toward those who honestly struggle to retrieve their past lives & become good. (*MTL* 3: 53)

Samuel Clemens first met Olivia Langdon in late December 1867. He proposed to her in early September 1868. Langdon accepted him on November 26, after rejecting him three times. They were formally engaged in February 1869, and married on February 2, 1870. Twenty-five months elapsed between introduction and wedding day.

This was quick work. Although the Langdon family clearly did not consider Clemens the savage that popular myth has described, and did, in fact, like him very much (probably right from the beginning), they also recognized how much he differed from the young men they knew. During the months between first proposing to Langdon and being accepted by her, and for several months thereafter, Clemens worked at relieving their anxieties, creating a set of themes and a series of feints designed to convince the entire Langdon family that he was a viable suitor. Because he also spent the majority of the time on the road giving lectures, or in Hartford seeing *The Innocents Abroad* through the editing and publication process, most of his communications with the Langdons took place on paper. Clemens wrote to Olivia Langdon every day, occasionally twice a day, and entreated her to respond in kind (she didn't). Beginning by presenting himself as a passionate suitor, verbally assaulting Langdon with his pleas, he gradually transformed himself into the steadfast fiancé, working out the details of their prospective lives together. In the process he convinced the entire family that despite the wildness of his frontier past, he had changed both spiritually and temperamentally. The courtship letters document the ways he negotiated these differences.[1]

Albert Bigelow Paine's biography of Mark Twain first established the story of the Langdon family's initial opposition, and eventual capitulation, to Clemens's suit. Much has been made – especially in the popular myth – of a putative conversation between Jervis Langdon and Clemens in regard to letters of recommendation that the family had requested from people familiar with Clemens's past. Apparently, many advised Jervis and Olivia Lewis Langdon not to allow their daughter to marry such a wild and undependable young man. According to Paine, when Jervis Langdon had determined that few of Clemens's friends would support him, he offered his own support: "Jervis Langdon held out his hand," claims Paine. " 'You have at least one [friend],' he said. '*I* believe in you. I know you better than *they* do.' "[2]

If this interview took place as Paine records it, Clemens must have sealed it into an unusually private part of his consciousness, for he never referred to it in letters written at the time. In fact, the letters of recommendation were such a source of anxiety for him that he struggled – long distance – to control them, fearing that they would undermine his suit. In the process, he worked out a rhetorical framework that evolved into his courtship's master trope. That framework demanded that the family ignore his past, rejoice in his present, and have faith in his future. "It is my desire as truly as yours," he wrote Jervis Langdon on December 29, 1868, "that sufficient time shall elapse to show you, beyond all possible question, what I *have been, what I am,* and what I am *likely to be.* Otherwise you could not be satisfied with me, nor I with myself" (*MTL* 2: 357).

Clemens had been a wild young man, a fact he readily admitted. "I have been, in times past, that which would be hateful in your eyes," he told Olivia Langdon on January 24, 1869. "But I have lived that life, and it is of the past. I do not live backwards. God does not ask of the returning sinner what he *has* been, but what he *is* and what he *will be.* And this is what you ask of me. If I must show what I am and prove what I *shall* be, I am content" (*MTL* 3: 74). Rhetorically, if not consciously, Clemens here fuses the loved one with God, a phenomenon not uncommon in his letters of this period and in Langdon's shortly after their marriage. Consciously, he was constructing a method through which the family could differentiate between appearance and deed, using imagery and references appealing to the Langdons' piety and to their sense of decorum and fiscal responsibility. "I think all my references can say I never did anything mean, false, or criminal," he told Jervis Langdon.

> They can say that the same doors that were open to me seven
> years ago are open to me yet; that *all* the friends I made in
> seven years, are still my friends; that wherever I have been I
> can go again – & enter in the light of day & hold my head up;
> that I never deceived or defrauded anybody, & don't owe a
> cent. And they can say that I attended to my business with due
> diligence, & made my own living, & never asked anybody to
> help me do it, either. All the rest they can say about me will
> be *bad.* I can tell the whole story myself, without mincing it, &
> will if they refuse. (*MTL* 2: 357–8)

This sounds as though his faults were limited to hard drinking (a serious fault to the abstemious Langdons and one that Clemens could understand through his experiences with his own teetotaling mother), smoking, late nights, and rough practical jokes. In fact, his sins were probably worse than that; according to Margaret Sanborn he probably slept with various servant women and prostitutes,[3] though I suspect that his fastidiousness would have prevented him from regular attendance at common whorehouses; in any case, chastity was probably not his strong suit. According to Andrew Hoffman, the crowd Clemens frequented in San Francisco also had a high tolerance for sexual ambiguity.[4] It is most likely that, between the mining country and San Francisco, he gained a sophisticated knowledge about all kinds of sexualities, even if his own participation was not excessive. In a culture celebrating "purity of mind," such knowledge made him culpable. Additionally, during his Nevada years Clemens lived in a frontier culture in which violence and cheating were rife; at the very least, he accepted mining stock in exchange for favorable reporting while he worked for the *Enterprise* (*MTL* 1: 259–61), and he was certainly aware of the many other forms of fraud common to the business of buying and selling mines. He also was witness to bloody brawls and probably a participant in some of them, and he was familiar with the murders and other furies of men and women living on the frontier. The result, he told Langdon rather bitterly, was to make him feel that

> I have been through the world's "mill" – I have traversed its ramifications from end to end – I have searched it, & probed it, & put it under the microscope, & I *know* it, through & through, & from back to back – its follies, it[s] frauds & its vanities – all by personal *experience* & not through dainty *theories* culled from nice moral books in luxurious parlors where temptation never comes & it is easy to be good & keep the heart warm & one's best impulses fresh & strong & uncontaminated – & now I know *how* to be a better man, & the *value* of so being, & when I say that I *shall* be, it is just the same as if I *swore* it! Now! (*MTL* 2: 290)

Clemens's bitterness, probably only partly feigned, stemmed from his sense that he was being judged by people – especially Langdon herself – who had neither experienced real temptation nor understood the cultural differences between the West and the East. "I think that much of my conduct on the Pacific Coast was not of a character to recommend me to the respectful regard of a high eastern civilization," he told Jervis Langdon, "but it was not considered blameworthy there, perhaps. We go according to our lights" (*MTL* 2: 357). Acknowledging the radical disparity between the standards for conduct in the bourgeois society of the East and the rough world of the western mining camps, Clemens pled cultural difference – and then hedged, for his final "perhaps" suggests that he knew that much of his conduct would not be condoned by genteel society in the West, either (nor was it, if the letters from western acquaintances who spoke against him are viable evidence). Then he introduced an argument that might have struck Jervis Langdon more immediately: "I was just what Charlie would have been, similarly circumstanced, & deprived of home influences," he continued. The Langdon son, Charles, whom Clemens had met on the *Quaker City* cruise and through whom he had been introduced to the family, was in a period of wild adolescence that Clemens knew was a subject of considerable concern to his parents. His not-so-subtle reminder to the father that the son's conduct did not meet the highest standards also supported his plea to be judged for his present and future conduct, not for that of his past. Treat me, Clemens's argument implied, as you hope another good family will treat your son when his wild oats are sown and his own courtship time arrives.

In this framework Clemens played with a number of prevailing ideas about right conduct that he knew his readers shared. One was integral to their common membership among the upwardly striving: that youthful errors should be forgiven once responsible adulthood was proved. In his letters, Clemens implied that whatever blots remained on his record, he was nevertheless honest and independent – character traits that, as any reader of Horatio Alger's novels knows, marked the era's ideal young man. Additionally, Clemens's "past, present, and future" structure fit into pietistic notions of sin, repentance, and redemption, while his reference to Charlie masterfully evoked references to prodigal sons. By appealing to the Langdons' bourgeois piety – that is, the complex of values that not only celebrated the repentant sinner but made good Christians partly responsible for his redemption – Clemens maneuvered his lover's parents into feeling responsible for helping him become the man they wanted him to be.

While Clemens's strategy to win Langdon's parents sought to earn their respect by evoking cultural definitions of responsible manhood, his strategy with Langdon herself was calculated to win not only her approval but also her heart and mind. Far more aggressive toward Olivia Langdon than toward her parents, Clemens's goal was to capture her attention and commandeer her loyalties. That required teaching her how to make him the center of her universe. One series of letters in particular shows how Clemens accomplished this, reshaping potentially destructive situations to further his goals. Langdon apparently described the contents of one of the California references in a letter she addressed to Clemens in Sparta, Wisconsin, in mid-January 1869. Clemens, however, did not go to Sparta, and therefore did not receive Langdon's letter until January 24. Meanwhile, he received other letters from her referring to the contents of the "Sparta letter," making him impatient to see the information it contained.

Apparently, the information was negative. In the Sparta letter, Langdon had reported on a reference from San Francisco, possibly from James S. Hutchinson, one of her father's former employees who, because he was then living in that city, had been requested to ask for references from two of Clemens's acquaintances there (*MTL* 3: 56–7, n6). His report apparently distressed the entire Langdon family, for while it chased him, Clemens agonized: "Oh, Livy, I *dread* the Sparta letter – for I know I shall find in it the evidence of your suffering. . . . How wrong & how unfair, it seems, that they [her parents] should be caused unhappiness for things which I alone should suffer for" (*MTL* 3: 53). He also, however, temporized, beginning to suggest that the letter would be more revelatory of its writer's faults than of his own:

I don't mind anything bad those friends have written your father about me, provided it was only true, but I *am* ashamed of

75

the friend whose friendship was so weak & so unworthy that he shrank from coming out openly & above-board & saying *all* he knew about me, good or bad – for there is nothing generous in his grieving insinuation – it is a covert stab, nothing better. We didn't want innuendoes – we want the *truth*. And I am honestly sorry he did not come out like a man & *tell* it.

Having begun undermining the correspondent's character, Clemens encouraged Langdon to trust her own judgment, by which he meant to believe in him despite the insinuations. "I am glad & proud that you resent the innuendo, my noble Livy. It was just like you. It fills me with courage & with confidence" (*MTL* 3: 52–3). By the time the Sparta letter finally reached him, Clemens had his strategy for dealing with it in hand: "It has come at last," he told Langdon on January 24. "And like most hidden terrors, I find myself reassured . . . & ready to cope with it. I sought eagerly for just one thing – if I could find that, I was safe. I did find it – *you still have faith in me.* That was enough – it is all I ask" (*MTL* 3: 73). The report that was apparently designed to destroy Clemens's chances with Langdon and her family had become, in his framework, a test of Langdon's faith in him, a faith that he scrutinized with the particularity of a Calvinist minister:

> By your two later letters I saw that you had faith in me . . . but what I yearned for at this particular moment was the evidence that your faith remained at its post when the storm swept over your heart. I believed I should find that evidence, for I did not think that your faith was the child of a passing fancy. . . . The belief was well grounded, & I am satisfied. (*MTL* 3: 73)

Ready to apologize profusely for his past, Clemens refused to let it control his future. By using the negative report as a test of Langdon's loyalty, he turned her doubt into faith, her womanly caution into determination to stand by him against the odds. In this struggle, Langdon, it seems, had been on trial, not he.

So much for Clemens's past. His present, as he revealed it to the family and to Langdon, was an extended moment of becoming, of hopeful apprenticeship to genuine piety and right conduct. Foremost in this picture was his determination to prove that he could become a Christian. After the official engagement, he would admit to scheming that Langdon would fall in love with him if he gave her leave to convert him: "My prophecy was correct," he wrote to his mother on February 5, 1869. "She said she never could or would love me – but she set herself the task of making a Christian of me. I said she would succeed, but that in the meantime she would unwittingly dig a matrimonial pit & end by tumbling into it – & lo! the prophecy is fulfilled" (*MTL* 2: 85). At the onset of his campaign, however, he presented himself as thoughtful, somewhat anguished, but eager to learn to love God. He also implied that he could not succeed without Langdon's unflagging interest.

> You say to me: "I shall pray for you daily." Not any words that ever were spoken to me have touched me like these . . . I have been thinking, thinking, thinking – & what I have arrived at, is the conviction that I would be less than a man if I went on in my old careless way while you were praying for me. . . . I beg that you will continue to pray for me – for I have a vague, far-away sort of idea that it may not be wholly in vain. In one respect, at least, it *shall* not be in vain – for I will so mend my conduct that I shall grow *worthier* of your prayers, & your good will & sisterly solicitude, as the days go by. Furthermore, (– it has taken me long to make up my mind to say these grave words . . .) I *will* "pray with you," as you ask. (*MTL* 2: 250–1)

For the next few months Clemens diligently applied himself to the process of becoming a Christian, even telling his family and "Mother" Fairbanks of his intentions. In his letters to Langdon he frequently returned to the prospect. "*Wait* on the Lord," he hymned in one meditation, much of it phrased in one extended sentence. "And so, conning my lesson with 'good courage' & with firm faith, I 'WAIT.' I 'wait' – in His own good time my hope will be crowned with its fruition. And *then*! my life will have an object! What an amazing value the thought gives to this life of mine, which was so perfectly valueless before!" He ends this peroration to himself with a moral designed to affect the sensibilities of his tutor: "Perhaps you may appreciate that last remark when I tell you that for many years, & up to much less than a year ago I absolutely loved to look upon dead men & envy them! I *couldn't* keep from envying them – & in *all* moods – joy & sorrow the same. I was well nigh a savage, Livy" (*MTL* 2: 329–30).

Throughout Clemens's written record of his efforts to become a Christian, he presents his struggle within the framework of the traditional Protestant conversion narrative; that is, he tells Langdon about his failures as well as his successes, his backsliding as well as his moments of hope. With the skill of a Jonathan Edwards, he records the course of his conversion, playing on Langdon's enculturation in what we can call the discourse of conversion – the widely recognized rhetoric that had evolved around Protestant conversion experiences and had become an index to moral character. Whether or not he ever read the masters of this genre, Clemens certainly knew the discourse from his childhood and from the ubiquitous religious tracts that were a staple of the American Protestant establishment. As with other traditional forms, he used this one with extraordinary skill. At the same time that he used and in many ways *believed in* both the form and the spiritual struggle it signaled, however, he also had ulterior motives. Whereas converts like Edwards prayed to God and recorded their struggles in order to edify posterity, Clemens prayed and recorded his struggles in order to seduce Langdon. The records of the struggles sound similar, but the ends are radically, even blasphemously, different: Edwards wrote to teach others how to be ready for grace, should God choose to bestow it; Clemens wrote to persuade one individual that she should become his deity and choose to bestow grace on him. Certainly not the first lover to fuse sexual and spiritual yearning, Clemens brilliantly appropriated the rhetoric of the conversion narrative in order to manipulate Langdon's religious beliefs.

That he was manipulating a known form does not, however, mean that Clemens was not (howsoever briefly) also genuinely struggling to become a Christian. Most latter-day readers of

Clemens's love letters have found it difficult to believe his professions, knowing first that he was a master manipulator of traditional forms, and second, that he gave up religion soon after the wedding – and that Langdon shortly followed suit. But we need to remember how much retrospection facilitates our skepticism. If we bracket our knowledge of subsequent events, reading these letters as Langdon would have read them and, perhaps more important, as Clemens wrote them, it is equally difficult not to be struck by their apparent sincerity. As with so much of his personal writing, Clemens's extraordinary ability to write himself into the role of the religious hopeful – to *perform* the role as he wrote it – was an exercise in self-creation. From this point of view Clemens's struggles to achieve faith were perfectly sincere, for, like many autobiographers, he constantly invented himself through language, becoming the narrator he inscribed on the page. Here, writing created the author, the self, rather than the reverse. As he recorded his efforts to know Jesus within a framework bearing its own rhetorical history of spiritual struggle, Clemens did not mask *as* the anguished religious apprentice so much as *become* him, riding highs and lows of hope and doubt. "I pray as one who prays with words," he forlornly told Langdon in October, soon after he had agreed to pray with her (*MTL* 2: 271). In December he was still struggling: "I lack the *chief* ingredient of piety," he confessed, "for I lack (almost always) the 'special moral emotion' – that inner sense which tells me that what I do I am doing *for love* of the Savior. I *can* be a Christian – I *shall* be a Christian – but when I feel as I feel today, it seems a far journey away" (*MTL* 2: 353).

At the same time he was recording his hopes and fears, however, Clemens was also pursuing his original goal. One strategy was to begin fusing the image of Langdon with that of Jesus. Despite Langdon's having cautioned him that he should "not believe in any mortal as you believe in your Savior" (*MTL* 2: 303), he argued that by letting him try to be good for love of her she was merely helping him know God. "You know the child must crawl before it walks – & I must do right for love of you while I am in the infancy of Christianity; & then I can do right for love of the Savior when I shall have gotten my growth" (*MTL* 2: 353–4), he pleaded. In passages such as this he used the rhetoric of spiritual love while refusing to heed its strictures. The prohibition against loving mortals as much as God exists to keep believers from confusing sacred and profane emotions. When Clemens assumed that Langdon would not refuse a love that figured her as "practice" for a burgeoning piety, he used his conversion process as a ploy in his courtship proceedings. Heedless of her warning, he maneuvered her into letting herself become the real focus of his worship.

In addition to casting his burgeoning relationship with God in traditional terms, Clemens vowed to abandon some of his worst habits if Langdon would consider his suit. Like all good Horatio Alger heroes, he aspired to clean living. For a time, he overcame his penchant for alcohol. "I drink no spirituous liquors any more," he wrote his sister, Pamela Moffett, in late November 1868. "I do nothing that is not thoroughly *right* – I am *rising*" (*MTL* 2: 295). He was not, however, yet ready to give up cigars: "I am reasonably afraid that you'll stop me from smoking, some day," he told Langdon in the same letter in which he asked her to be his model for Jesus. "But if ever you do, you will do it with such a happy grace that I shall be swindled into the notion that I didn't *want* to smoke any more, anyhow!" (*MTL* 2: 354). Although he mentions his struggle with liquor most frequently, he also notes that he is trying to overcome his temper, always volatile and prone to explode under stress: "I grew so exasperated, at last, that I shouted to the door keeper to close the doors & not open them again on *any* account," he confessed to Langdon in a letter recounting a bad night on the lecture circuit. "And now I have to pray for forgiveness for these things – & unprepared, Livy, for the bitterness is not all out of my bad, foolish heart yet" (*MTL* 3: 31). Perhaps because he diligently reported his backsliding, he seemed to feel that he made progress; significantly, his victories over himself and over Langdon's resistance to his suit seem to have come in tandem. "Now I never swear," he told

Langdon's mother just after becoming formally engaged. "I never taste wine or spirits upon *any* occasion whatsoever; I am orderly, & my conduct is above reproach in a worldly sense; & finally, I now claim that I am a Christian. I claim it, & it only remains to be seen if my bearing shall show that I am justly entitled to so name myself" (*MTL* 3: 90). Creating his own trope out of the differences among past, present, and future, and using the potent argument for his future implicit in both the framework of the conversion narrative and the narrative of upward mobility, by the time the engagement was made public Clemens had created a self that functioned successfully within the religious and moral ideology of his fiancée and her parents.

In addition to reconstructing his present, Clemens's letters to Langdon forecast his future, especially as it would be if she agreed to continue inspiring him. Dismissing the past and eliding the present, he concluded his comments on the Sparta letter by assuring Langdon that "I know that howsoever black they may have painted me, you will steadfastly believe I am not so black *now*, & never *will* be, any more." And he established the tension between sin and repentance that would guide his relationship with her for the next thirty-five years: "I will be just as good as ever I *can* be, & will never cause you sorrow any more" (*MTL* 3: 53). In this more secularly oriented letter he overtly named Langdon as the focus of his desires, his reason for conforming to bourgeois values: "Married to you, I would never desire to roam again while I lived," he told her, apparently in reference to her parents' concern that he had no fixed abode. Rather, he implied that he would cleave to Langdon and that any roaming he did would be with her, through time, not space.

> When we are married we shall be as happy, as kings – unpretending, substantial members of society, with no fuss or show or nonsense about us . . . & so developing all of good & worthy that is in our natures, walk serenely down the grand avenues of Time, never sorrowing to see the drifting years dropping away one by one to join the buried ages, but glad to know that

each passing year left its welcome sign that we were drawing nearer & nearer to that home of rest & peace where we shall know & love each other through all the vague tremendous centuries of eternity. (*MTL* 3: 58–9)

From wanderer to devoted husband to inhabitant of Heaven; rhetorically, Clemens showed Langdon his future and sought to convince her that her place lay with him.

In addition to the overarching framework of past, present, and future, with its emphasis on religious and moral conversion and its projection of married life into old age and a Christian heaven, in his letters to the Langdons, Clemens established a series of subthemes that both articulated and attempted to resolve the various tensions that he felt with them. One goal was to convince the family that he was steady, stable, and able to deal with financial affairs. At the same time that he was assuring Langdon that he was ready to reform, he was busily assuring his authority figures that he was prepared to settle down. "This thing of settling down for life is the solemnest matter that has ever yet come into my calculations," he told Mary Fairbanks in April 1869. "I am not inclined to get in a sweat about it, or make a move without looking well into it first. I must not make a mistake in this thing" (*MTL* 3: 195). To his prospective father-in-law he showed his business side in a December 2, 1868, letter:

> John Russell Young . . . tells me that the price of *Tribune* shares is $7,000 each, & none in market just now. There are 100 shares, altogether, & a share yields $1,000 a year . . . He wants me to buy – told him I would take as many shares as I could mortgage my book for, & as many more as I could pay for with labor of hand & brain. (*MTL* 2: 298)

"I propose to earn money enough some way or other," he told Olivia Lewis Langdon, with more humor than he had used in his letter to her husband, "to buy a remunerative share in a newspaper of high standing, & then instruct & elevate & civilize the public through its columns, & my wife (to be,) will superintend the domestic economy, furnish ideas & sense, erase improprieties from the manuscript, & read proof. That is all she will have to do. Mere pastime for a person of her calibre" (*MTL* 3: 92).

Clemens also showed his appreciation for his new family by using his newspaper connections, one of his few sources of power, to help them. On the way to Alice Hooker's wedding in June 1869, Clemens used his influence with the New York *Tribune* to help his prospective father-in-law obtain money owed him by the city of Memphis (*MTL* 3: 265, n2). Additionally, after he became one of the editors of the Buffalo *Express*, that paper suddenly ceased espousing the public's side in a dispute between a coal monopoly (in which Jervis Langdon's company participated) and the people of Buffalo (*MTL* 3: 306, n3). Clemens may have been willing to "reform" many of his Nevada ways, but he apparently did not find it necessary to forget how to use his newspaper connections to help big business. It may be indicative of the business mores of the era that this family, which prided itself on personal and business morality, did not seem to have found a moral fault in his interference on their behalf.

One of Clemens's trickiest negotiations involved his relationship with his prospective father-in-law. A successful businessman, Jervis Langdon demonstrated his care for community and family through his involvement in civic and domestic affairs, from his covert participation in financing the local branch of the Underground Railway before the Civil War to his positions on the boards of the local orphans' home and the Academy of Science after the war. He also attended Wednesday-night prayer meetings with his wife and spent evenings at home with family and friends. Alice Hooker's letters attest to his centrality in the family life and his informality in the family circle; in her missive to her mother describing the Langdons' conservatory she notes that "in one corner of the conservatory is an aquarium full of fishes, which is Mr. Langdon's special delight. He gets excused from desert [*sic*] every day so that 'he may go and play with the fishes' " (April 19, 1867). Alice's mother also felt warmly (exceedingly warmly) about Jervis Langdon. In one letter to her daughters, written while she and the Langdons were vacationing in Saratoga and

Alice and Mary were home in Hartford, she averred, "I tell you – this is a man among men. I never knew him till now – his modesty has kept in chains till quite lately & it is since I first knew him that he has come to the self estimate that gives him the power & interest I now recognize."[5]

Clemens and Jervis Langdon seem to have liked one another; nevertheless, Clemens, in the delicate position of poor suitor and (still poor) prospective son-in-law, treated the older man with great care, both in his letters to him and his references to him in letters to his daughter. In his letters to Jervis Langdon he chose to be forthright and manly. Responding to an apparently critical letter from the older man, for example, he remarked, "I am safely past that tender age when one cannot take his food save that it be masticated for him beforehand, – & I would much prefer to suffer from the lean incision of an honest lancet than from a sweetened poison. Therefore it is even as you say: I have 'too much good sense' to blame you for that part of the letter. Plain speaking does not hurt one" (*MTL* 2: 357). Interestingly, that Clemens originally began the last line to read: "Plain speaking only increases one's esteem & respect for the speaker," but crossed most of the words out, perhaps because he was afraid they would seem toadying. Throughout his letters to Jervis Langdon he struck the note of calm self-possession and, occasionally, humor.

To others, and especially to Olivia Langdon, he referred to Jervis Langdon respectfully. Beneath the respect, however, one occasionally hears a note of annoyance at his prospective father-in-law's own pranks, especially when they interrupted the tête-à-têtes that Clemens considered sacrosanct. "Mr. L. has had plenty of fun to-day, breaking in on our private drawing-room confidences under pretense of measuring the room to see if it is large enough for *three*," he grumbled to Mary Fairbanks on Thanksgiving Day, 1868, just after Langdon had agreed to marry him. "And for all the old gentleman is so concerned he knows he has not been so jolly himself for months, or had such noble opportunities for poking fun at helpless people" (*MTL* 2: 284). A month later he commented, "Mr. Langdon is well again, & was perfectly jolly – bothered us & interrupted us all he could – & appeared to enjoy it" (*MTL* 2: 349). Here, the father's interruptions can be read as veiled threats as well as playful jokes, like those of many men whose daughters have suddenly manifested a sexual interest in another man. Even after the marriage Jervis Langdon reminded Clemens of his place as first in his daughter's affections: "Samuel, I love your wife," he wrote to the couple from Richmond on April 2, 1870, continuing

> and she loves me. I think it only fair that you should know it but you need not flare up, I loved her before you did and she loved me before she did you & has not ceased since. I see no way but for you to "make the most of it" – my wife sends much love. Your father J. Langdon. (*MTL* 4: 109, n1)

By that time, Clemens had won and did not need to defend himself. Earlier, he had been cautious: "It was just like Mr. Langdon in his most facetious mood, to say he would kill me if I wasn't good to you," he had noted to Olivia early in 1869 (*MTL* 3: 46). Nevertheless, he worried about his tone to Jervis Langdon. "I wrote your father yesterday in answer to his letter about making haste slowly," he told her on December 30, 1868. "But I wish I hadn't written him that Christmas letter from Lansing, for I fear he does not know me as well as you do, Livy, & I am apt to pain him with my heedless way of writing, though you know I don't mean any harm. I love him too well & reverence him too much to pain him wantonly" (*MTL* 2: 364). Muted but still evident, Clemens's anxiety about his relationship with his father-in-law sounds a recurrent note in his negotiations with his new family.[6]

Another theme running throughout Clemens's letters of this time – and one not at all muted – concerns his "theft" of Langdon from her family. Although he vowed that he would no more wander, Clemens was not about to settle in Elmira, and both Langdon and her family made it clear that the prospect of her removal caused them considerable pain.

> I cannot, & need not, detail to you the utter surprise & almost astonishment with which Mr Langdon & myself listened to Mr Clemens [*sic*] declaration to us, of his love for our precious child, and how at first our parental hearts said no. – to the bare thought of such a stranger, mining in our hearts for the possession of one of the few jewels we have,

Olivia Lewis Langdon wrote in anguish to Mary Fairbanks early in December 1868 (*MTL* 2: 286, n3). Here the mother figures her daughter in the language of material possession, a trope that Clemens developed by characterizing himself as a thief, thus establishing another set of tensions between himself and Langdon's parents.

> Livy, I could not tell your honored father & mother how deeply I felt for them, & how heartless it seemed in me to come, under cover of their trusting, generous hospitality, & try to steal away the sun out of their domestic firmament & rob their fireside heaven of its angel . . . they could have upbraided me for my treachery . . . yet there was nothing criminal in my *intent*,

he wrote Langdon in late November 1868 (*MTL* 2: 290).

As in his insistence that Jervis and Olivia Lewis Langdon judge him not by his past but by the future, which he fully intended to be exemplary, here Clemens demanded that the family judge his act through *his* point of view, that is, through his love for Langdon, rather than through their own. At the same time, however, he continued to characterize himself as "treacherous" and a "thief." In this vocabulary Langdon, the object of both parties' desire, became the value through which they demonstrated their relative powers. Initially dominant, Jervis and Olivia Lewis Langdon "possessed" this "jewel" in addition to their house, mines, mills, and other signs of material wealth. By the end of the courtship, Clemens had succeeded in wresting it from them, a victory that, though he continued to apologize for it profoundly, also boosted his self-esteem: "I haven't yet got over a secret thrill of vanity when I see the dear old familiar hand on a letter for me," he told Langdon on September 7, 1869.

I always feel proud . . . a year ago, I *was* so proud to get a letter from you in Cleveland . . . & *now,* why I can hardly comprehend that it is actually *I* that get a letter *every day* from Livy – & she is *mine* – my own Livy for time & eternity – never to be taken from me by any hand but that of the arch Destroyer. . . . You are unspeakably precious to me . . . a blessing before which all other earthly treasures are dross & worthless. (*MTL* 3: 344)

By figuring Langdon in the language of possession, both parties to this battle revealed their participation in yet another discursive arena: one in which all phenomena became objects of value to be rated and exchanged. Like books, which they consumed as a mandatory part of their growth into the middle class, the Langdon family's material universe included relatives and close friends. Engaged, loving, and caring Victorian Americans, they also viewed their intimates through others' eyes, judging their relative worth and their possibilities for exchange. In this economy parents reluctant to see their children marry placed a high value on their offsprings' exchange, forcing suitors to work hard to earn their reward. When the actual financial status of parent and suitor was also unequal, as it certainly was between Clemens and the Langdons, the struggle became even more intense, always figuring the poorer antagonist as an intruder into the closed world of the well-to-do. Clemens's professions of pride in his new fiancée, then, reflect his feelings that he had triumphed in an alien marketplace. Acknowledging his status as intruder, he basked in the fact that "I have stolen away the brightest jewel that ever adorned an earthly home" (*MTL* 3: 137).

After such a struggle, Clemens constantly needed to reassure himself that it was all worthwhile, that the object of great price was also of great value. In the nineteenth-century marital marketplace, women's value lay in their sexual purity, mental chastity, moral rectitude, and good sense – in addition, of course, to their looks, their money, and their domestic skills. Before the marriage, Clemens professed most interest in Langdon's mental and moral qualities, especially as they contrasted with his own. He harped on her virtues so insistently that at times he seemed to be wooing

Samuel L. Clemens, *c.* 1870. The Mark Twain House, Hartford, Connecticut.

Olivia Langdon Clemens, *c.* 1872. The Mark Twain House, Hartford, Connecticut.

her through rank flattery. "I love to believe that you are always right, Livy," he told her in a typical passage (*MTL* 3: 58). Despite her protests, Clemens insisted on treating Langdon as his superior, at least in matters that pertained to her experience: "You are as strong in these things as I am weak & bewildered," he wrote her about his struggles to overcome selfishness (*MTL* 2: 364). "Now please *don't* feel hurt when I praise you, Livy, for I know that in so doing I speak only the truth. At last I grant you one fault – & it is *self-depreciation*. . . . And yet, after all, your self-depreciation is a virtue & a merit, for it comes of the absence of egotism, which is one of the gravest of faults," (*MTL* 2: 3). Invidiously comparing his own self-centeredness to Langdon's ability to think of others first, Clemens plays here both with one of the chief characteristics of the good woman of the nineteenth century and with Protestant Christianity's insistence that true union with Christ can come only after the soul has been emptied of all selfish preoccupations. In praising Langdon's selflessness, he presents her as an exemplary woman and Christian, thus assuring both of them that she is, in pietistic parlance, a "pearl of great price" – a woman worth the trouble it took to get and keep her.[7]

In addition to erecting grand structures for figuring their relationship, Clemens also tried to build a basis for their daily lives together by responding to Langdon's ideas and sympathizing with her experiences. In response to her description of a young man who had shown his contempt for women, for instance, he carefully separated himself from such misogynists. "I have seen your young gentlemen women-haters often – I know them intimately," he told her on January 14, 1869. He proceeded to characterize them as "whelps with vast self-conceit," "day-dreamers," and men whose "pet vanity is to be considered 'men of the world,' " even though "they generally know about as much of the world as a horse knows about metaphysics." Interestingly, Clemens's focus shifts in the paragraph he devotes to this type; beginning in a tone of sympathy for Langdon, who had apparently suffered some discomfort from the presence of the man she described, he becomes involved in his character description, ending by being far more concerned about the character of the generic misogynist than in his effect on women. "They are powerfully sustained in their woman-hating. . . . They are coarse, & vulgar, & mean," he tells his fiancée comfortingly, and then pursues his narrative to a conclusion far closer to his interests in alienated individuals than to her interest in why some men hate women: "When *sense* dawns upon these creatures . . . they are full forty years old . . . & they sigh to feel that those years & the pleasures they might have borne, are wasted," he continues. He concludes by expressing Christian sympathy for the tragedy: "I *do* pity a woman-hater with all my heart. The spleen he suffers is beyond comprehension" (*MTL* 3: 39–40). Here Clemens responds to his fiancée's observations by framing the incident she has recounted in a traditional interpretive framework. By making misogynists into a specialized form of misanthrope, Clemens can express sympathy, show that he is beginning to understand Christian principles governing human conduct, and avoid actually confronting the effect such men have on the women they encounter. Never really able to assume a woman's point of view, Clemens's acute analysis of men who hate women rests, in the end, within the male viewpoint, examining the harm they do to themselves, not to the women they malign.

Clemens's paragraph about misogynists occurs in one of many letters that are clearly written, topic by topic, in response to Langdon's own remarks. One of these topics concerns the nature of husbands. Scattered throughout Clemens's missives are responses suggesting that Langdon was actively studying married men, trying to determine which model Clemens would best fit. But Clemens tried to dissuade her from comparing him with other men of her acquaintance. "Livy, dear, *don't* measure me with all the mean husbands in the world," he begged her on January 22, 1869. "I'm *not* mean, & heartless, & unloving – I am not, indeed, Livy – as truly as I live, I am not the counterpart of that man you speak of" (*MTL* 3: 64). Written within the same month, Clemens's responses to Langdon's description of a misogynist and to a woman married to a cold man suggest that Langdon was studying other people's marriages carefully, paying especial attention to husbands' sensitivities to their wives' feelings. Perceiving this, Clemens rushed to assure her that he cared how she felt. "When you are heavy-hearted, write at once," he implored her, "& let me put my arms about you, darling, & comfort you . . . for this is the true office of love" (*MTL* 3: 77).

Clemens's sympathy for the "jewel" he was about to steal was most evident in his letters that tried to comfort Langdon on her imminent departure from home. Never did Clemens mention that for a good part of her adolescent illness Langdon was separated from her family while living in sanitariums, an experience that must have taught her how to live without her parents, if not how to be fully independent. Rather, he participated in the fantasy that she has never left her parental roof. He also turns Langdon's expressions of foreboding into the same kind of rhetorical construct that he was so expert at creating for himself. In one letter he responded to a passage of Langdon's – in which she lamented leaving home – by comparing the pathos of her words to a passage from *Tristram Shandy*. "You touch one as nearly as Lawrence Sterne," he told her. Significantly, the passage to which he referred is one of the few in *Tristram Shandy* that is *not* ironic; it features a brave but foolish old man whose courage is registered in heaven, if not on earth. In comparing Langdon's writing to Sterne's, Clemens explicitly figured her as an artist, an expert at the literary representation of feeling. As soon as he had praised her writing, however, he began to reconstruct his own experiences of leaving home, in effect competing with her description. "You shall never know the chill that comes upon me sometimes when I feel that long absence has made me a stranger in my own home," he told her. "I can only *look in* upon their world without entering; & I turn me away with a dull aching consciousness that long exile has lost to me that haven of rest, that pillow of weariness, that refuge from care, & trouble & pain, that type & symbol of heaven, HOME." He then turned from himself back to Langdon: "But *you* shall not know this great blank, this awful vacancy," he assured her. Rather, with their friends and relatives frequently visiting, and a home "modeled after the old home"; most of all, with Langdon's Jesus to guide them: "Turn toward the Cross & be comforted – I turn with you. . . . The peace of God shall rest upon us, & all will be well" (*MTL* 2: 345–6). From Langdon's writing, to Sterne's, to his own, Clemens bridged the gap between Olivia's fears and his own hopes by establishing a standard for the rhetorical representation of emotion, then by praising Langdon's expertise at it, then by showing that he, too, could write feelingly about separation. Entering Langdon's emotional landscape also meant, for him, participating, even competing, in its literary representation.

Love Texts

Clemens's references to *Tristram Shandy* were not unusual in his communications with Langdon. Their numerous references to books are one of the most interesting aspects of the letters they exchanged. Readers of the courtship letters have often noticed that Clemens used particular texts as courting devices, but there is increasing evidence that Langdon did exactly the same thing, with an equal consciousness that they were weapons in a series of premarital battles, including a debate over appropriate reading for women and for men. Like the rhetorical feints Clemens developed to teach his prospective in-laws how to interpret him, the arguments Langdon and Clemens conducted over their readings of other writers' works reveal their personal agendas for their lives together. As with most couples, these agendas were not always compatible.

As we reevaluate Langdon and her circle we begin to understand how serious a reader she actually was. In fact it is possible to argue that she valued books just below God, that Clemens knew this about her, and that he simultaneously shared her passion and used it in his own interest.

> When we are serene & happy old married folk, we will sit together & con . . . books all the long pleasant evenings, & let the

great world toil & struggle & nurse its pet ambitions & glorify
its poor vanities beyond the boundaries of our royalty – we will
let it lighten & thunder, & blow its gusty wrath about our win-
dows & our doors, but never cross our sacred threshold,

he told Langdon in mid-January 1869. Constructing his favorite
image of marriage from the cultural association of good women
with houses, here he furnished his and Langdon's married life
with books. "Only Love & Peace shall inhabit there, with you &
I, their willing vassals," he continued.

> And I will read:
> "The splendor falls on castle walls,
> And snowy summits old in story" –
> & worship Tennyson, & you will translate Aurora Leigh & be
> gentle & patient with me & do all you can to help me under-
> stand what the mischief it is all about. And we will follow the
> solemn drum-beat of Milton's stately sentences; & the glittering
> pageantry of Macaulay's, & the shuddering phantoms that
> come & go in the grim march of Poe's unearthly verses; & bye
> & bye drift dreamily into fairy-land with the magician laureate
> & hear "the horns of elfland faintly blowing." And out of the
> Book of Life you shall call the wisdom that shall make our lives
> an anthem void of discord & our deeds a living worship of the
> God that gave them. (*MTL* 3: 25–6)

This passage illustrates Clemens's extraordinary skill at fusing as-
sociations and building a fictional universe from the fusion. Clos-
ing out the cold world, he and Langdon would live in the universe
of great literature, including, at its apex, the Bible, which Langdon, as befit her better understanding of that text, would expound. She would also expound *Aurora Leigh*, one of her favorite
works; here, however, Clemens could not resist a dig at what he
considered to be its obscurity. His function would be to listen to
her teachings and to do the reading aloud. Buttressed by their
favorite books, he implied, they would create a haven of peace,
an escape from the world, a place in which Langdon's superior
intellect would reign.

Clemens and Langdon's exchanges over books in the courtship letters is one of the best illustrations we have of their relationship in those early days. Although almost none of Langdon's letters survive, Clemens's responses to her give a fairly good indication of what she had written. "I am so glad you like the 'exquisite' book, Livy – & if I only had it now I could mark it as it *should* be marked, I think. I was afraid, before, because I feared you might dislike [it]. . . . I shall always like that book, now, because it makes you think of *me*" (*MTL* 2: 369). The "exquisite" book is Coventry Patmore's *The Angel in the House,* which Clemens had discovered in October and had been writing to her about ever since. A book-length narrative poem written in four parts, *The Angel in the House* functioned, as Carol Christ has noted, both to define the image of the good woman in Victorian culture and to help Victorian men recognize the normalcy of their own feelings of inadequacy.[8] It clearly spoke to Clemens; he often referred to it and sometimes quoted from it in his correspondence with Langdon. One letter in particular shows him using the poem to reveal his own sense of weakness, much as he used passages from the Bible to show his struggles to know God. Castigating himself for "not making a progress toward a better life worthy any one's faith," he admitted to feeling "unmanned" and first quoted, then heavily scratched out (because "it might have made you unhappy"), lines from Patmore that project a male speaker in a moment of regression and despair: "My Mother, would I might / But be your little child to-night, / And feel your arms about me fold, / Against this loneliness & cold!" (*MTL* 2: 311–12).[9] Over the course of their courtship letters (and, in fact, in later years, for he referred to this poem many times during his correspondence with his wife) Clemens took *The Angel in the House* as a guiding text, an accurate description of his states of mind and the status of their relationship. "I have found in the 'exquisite' book to-night a passage which is the soul & spirit of what I have been trying to tell you with tongue & pen. It is *confirmation*. It is prophecy," he told her in his next letter. The passage to which Clemens referred clearly pertains to the happiness pursuant on marriage, even after initial hesitations. "Read it, Livy, & you will see yourself in it," he continued, "& you will see that you need have no doubts & no misgivings when you wish that I shall succeed." Later in the same letter, however, he decided that she should not yet read the book, perhaps because it would reveal his game plan to her: "Livy, I don't like the 'exquisite' book, now, as I did before. I don't want you to read it now. I will keep it for you, & you shall read it another time." Ignoring his change of mind, she read it, and from then on his letters show that they were actively discussing it. "Ladies don't usually like those books, Livy," he noted at the end of December, "because those same books praise them so much, maybe." Despite this recognition, he proceeded to equate his "lady" and the object of Patmore's protagonist's affections: "Honoria is a great-souled, self-sacrificing, noble woman like you (I can see you in everything she does) & she is so happy in the weal of others & so compassionate of their woes. And she is so thoughtful, & so tender, & so exquisitely womanly" (*MTL* 2: 343). Perhaps the ladies did not like such books because they created impossible exemplars. It is clear from Clemens's letters that Langdon frequently objected to his idealization of her; if Honoria was his model of the perfect woman, Langdon was wise to try convincing him that she was imperfect. Despite her protests, Patmore's text, which traces a relationship from courtship through old age, remained one of Clemens's favorite fictional examples of what a marriage should be.

The books that Langdon chose as marriage manuals were also idealized, but unlike Clemens's favorite texts, which demanded exemplary behavior from women but permitted men their mortal weaknesses, Langdon's idealized men, too. In the letter in which he told Langdon that he did not want her to read Patmore yet, Clemens mentioned other books that they were reading in tandem. "I forgive *you*, you know, for forbidding me to read the 'Home Life,' " he told her, "– & so I shall read 'A Life for a Life' instead – & shall like it, no doubt, because you do" (*MTL* 2: 313–14). Perhaps Langdon forbade him to read *The Home Life: In the Light of Its Divine Idea* (1867), by James Baldwin Brown, because it, like Patmore's poem, idealized women, creating standards of conduct and spirituality impossible for ordinary mortals to achieve. Instead she encouraged him to read *A Life for a Life*, by Dinah Maria Mulock Craik, a popular English writer from whose works Langdon had already quoted in her commonplace book. *A Life for a Life* tells the story of a young woman's courtship by an older man. Written in the form of two diaries, it examines the relationships between sin and repentance, past and future, and men and women. Questioning the finality of society's judgments, it suggests that both women and men can overcome past mistakes – even grave ones like murder and sexual promiscuity – and go on to happy lives, including marriage. Certainly reassuring to Clemens when read in light of his own past, *A Life for a Life* also demonstrated Langdon's interest in the relationship between married men and women, for unlike Baldwin's book, it called for equal moral standards for both sexes. Not an explicitly feminist text, *A Life for a Life* nevertheless does envision Christian marriage from a woman's point of view. As we have seen, the record of Langdon's writings suggests that she did not challenge prevailing gender definitions. She did, however, seek to equalize the demands for upright moral behavior on men as well as women, and she was drawn to texts that articulated women's views even when they spoke from the most conservative stance.

Clemens's brief references to these two texts signal the way that he and Langdon used books to communicate their expectations for each other. In the game of "my text, your text," we unfortunately know far more about Clemens's choices than about Langdon's. Nevertheless, indirect references to her tastes, such as Clemens's remark just cited, as well as the evidence left in her commonplace book and letters, suggest that Langdon was trying to teach him to appreciate the viewpoint about men, women, and marriage that she was in the process of constructing for herself. In light of her framework, Clemens's jokes about *Aurora Leigh* are telling. Remarks such as "Get your Browning ready – for lo, I come like a lamb to the Slaughter! You know very well that I enjoyed my lessons before, notwithstanding I couldn't get the gas-lamps right" (*MTL* 2: 274) work two ways: on the one hand, they indicate that Clemens was willing to use her desire to "convert" him to further his suit, even when the conversion was to forms of literature (about which he actually cared far more than about forms of religion). Hence, he listened to her lectures on *Aurora Leigh* even though he had no intention of learning to like Elizabeth Barrett Browning's poems.

On the other hand, such remarks also reveal that Langdon was earnestly trying to explicate a text that she felt would be important to their understanding of their relationship. Although she was neither as literal-minded as Clemens portrayed her in his letters nor as devoid of humor as popular myth has broadcast, Langdon was certainly earnest in her desire to be honest with Clemens about her own tastes, beliefs, and expectations. The basis of *Aurora Leigh*'s immense popularity among nineteenth-century women lay in its exploration of the possibility that women could regard themselves as independent beings, and that men and women could enter companionate marriages. Its lengthy narrative passages on the psychological and social evolutions necessary for these steps are as meditative and as didactic as Young's *Night Thoughts*, which we know was also one of Langdon's favorite works. Both require patient literary exegesis, the kind of reading that scholars, not artists like Twain, enjoy. Like her interests in positivist science, Langdon's willingness to perform these tasks is perhaps one of our best clues to her intellectual type. They also tell us that she took life very seriously and used books to teach her how to deal with it.

Although he both teased and valued her for her seriousness, Clemens rejected Langdon's implication that he, too, should patiently explicate dense, literary texts. Rather, he professed to value them solely for what they revealed of Langdon's abilities: "I shall always have an affection for Browning because she exhibits your brains so well," he dryly advised his fiancée on February 13, 1869. "It always makes me proud of you when you assault one of her impenetrable sentences and tear off its shell and bring its sense to light" (*MTL* 3: 95). In critiquing *Aurora Leigh* for its style rather than its themes, Clemens sidestepped Langdon's request that he engage one of her favorite literary works on her level. Certainly *The Angel in the House* and *Aurora Leigh* suggest a basic disparity in Langdon's and Clemens's views about marriage. If virtuous Honoria and suffering Felix, protagonists of Patmore's poem, were Clemens's models for Livy and Sam, and independent Aurora and arrogant Romney were Langdon's, it should have been clear to both parties that there was much to be negotiated during the courtship period.

In keeping with their disparate views about the roles of men and women in marriage and in life, Clemens and Langdon also seem to have disputed about the role of knowledge in the construction of a woman's virtue. If purity of mind was a virtue for men in Victorian America, it was a necessity for women. Increasingly, Clemens sought to guide Langdon's reading, keeping sexual and scatological passages from her. It is not entirely clear whether she resisted him. One wishes even more, here, that Langdon's letters to Clemens about reading had survived, or that she had left lists of books read in a diary, as her mother did. Clearly, Langdon had read widely and thoughtfully before she met Clemens, in books ranging from primary texts to literary histories. Evidence from her commonplace book, for instance, shows that she had read Thackeray *on* Swift; we do not know, however, whether she actually read Swift himself. She had read Mühlbach on Frederick the Great but not yet Carlyle; she had read much of Shakespeare, probably in unexpurgated editions; she had read many of the approved British and American novels of the nineteenth century. None of this information indicates whether she found some of the material offensive; the only judgment of this type indicated in her writing is a reference to *The Scarlet Letter* as "unhealthful" in a letter she wrote to Alice Hooker more than a year before she met Clemens (June 7, 1867). For the rest, there is no evidence either way – she simply does not mention sexual or scatological passages. Rather, she seems to have just read everything that interested her.

Clemens, on the other hand, was obsessed with the idea that

literature might soil Langdon's purity. In this he aligned himself with the most conservative guardians of the nation's morals, those who believed that literature could corrupt readers, especially young women. As Nina Baym demonstrates in *Novels, Readers, and Reviewers: Responses to Fiction in Antebellum America*, these guardians of public virtue reflected the contradictory notions that, on the one hand, young women were so innately virtuous that they would automatically reject the coarse and the indelicate, and on the other, that they would be so taken in by their reading that the act of reading alone would corrupt them.[10] With this, of course, Clemens's obsession with Langdon's intellectual purity was part and parcel of his figuring her as an expensive object whose worth he did not want to depreciate. In his letters, Clemens unwittingly undermined his declarations of faith in Langdon's intellectual superiority by continually cautioning her about reading books that would sully her womanhood. In his letter comparing her writing to a portion of *Tristram Shandy*, for instance, Clemens presented the novel as an exemplary text, praising its depiction of Toby's rebellion against heaven's apparent decree. Throughout, he discussed *Tristram Shandy* as if Langdon were familiar with it. At the same time, however, he claimed to hope she had not read it: "Do you remember Uncle Toby & the wounded soldier?" he began. He continued, "(I hope not, because the book is coarse, & I would not have you soil your pure mind with it)" (*MTL* 2: 344).

In a similar tease – tease because he wrote excitedly about a text that was clearly interesting, then forbade her to read it – Clemens discussed Swift:

> I have been reading – I *am* reading – Gulliver's Travels, & am much more charmed with it than I was when I read it last, in boyhood – for now I can see what a scathing satire it is upon the English government, whereas, before, I only gloated over its prodigies & its marvels. Poor Swift – under the placid surface of this simply-worded book flows the full tide of his venom – the turbid sea of his matchless hate.

Beginning with this retrospective analysis, Clemens began to try to reconcile his recognition that Langdon, always interested in history and in literature that dealt with it, would find *Gulliver* attractive, with his conviction that Swift's "venom" would offend her delicacy. "You would not like the volume, Livy," he began, then quickly amended himself, "that is, a part of it. Some of it you would. If you would like to read it, though, I will mark it & tear it until it is fit for your eyes – for portions of it are very coarse & indelicate. I am sorry enough that I didn't ask you to let me prepare Don Quixote for your perusal, in the same way." He then claimed that the idea of her reading Cervantes unedited pained him so much that he urged her not to finish it. "You are as pure as snow, & I would have you always so – untainted, untouched even by the impure thoughts of others." Once embarked on this theme he found it difficult to stop. "Your purity is your most uncommon & most precious ornament," he continued. "Preserve it, Livy. Read nothing that is not *perfectly* pure . . . neither [*Don Quixote*] nor Shakspeare [*sic*] are proper books for virgins to read until some hand has culled them of their grossness . . . I did not mean to write a sermon, but still I have done it. However . . . it was a matter that lay near my heart" (*MTL* 3: 132–3).

It is easy to infer from this letter that Langdon had read *Don Quixote* unexpurgated. We do not know if she took Clemens's strictures seriously. One wants to believe that she did not, and certainly the independence she showed about reading suggests that she frequently disobeyed her literary mentor. In any case, Clemens did not let up on his preachings, at least before their wedding. "I am now reading Gil Blas, but am not marking it," he told her on December 27, 1869. "If you have not read it you need not. It would sadly offend your delicacy, & I prefer not to have that dulled in you. It is a woman's chief ornament" (*MTL* 3: 440). Like his comments about Cervantes a year earlier, this last reference to reading and delicacy shows Clemens in a moment of making his expectations clear: he wanted a woman who conformed to his culture's idea of modesty and chastity, in mind as well as body. Written in haste, this last letter lacks the lover's finesse that sugar-coated his censoriousness in the early missive. In the end, Clemens wanted Langdon to avoid reading corrupting material not because it would hurt her but because it would damage her and thus hurt *him* by decreasing her value (the value of the "jewel" he had stolen) in his and the world's eyes.

Less ominously, Clemens and Langdon also used literature, often marginally annotated, to make love long-distance. Certainly Clemens's marginal "marks" functioned as love notes and as interpretive guides, and Langdon accepted and valued them as such. This custom continued into their marriage, including the use of margins for love messages: "Clara and I have commenced 'Their Wedding Journey,' " Langdon wrote Clemens on December 31, 1871. "And I cannot help constantly wishing that you had marked it for me, I think maybe you would have said some nice sweet things in the margins that would have entitled it to a place in the green box [a place where she kept her treasures]. There are such exceedingly prettie [*sic*] love touches in it – I think I will have to get you to mark it yet some time" (December 30, 1871). He did mark Oliver Wendell Holmes's *Autocrat at the Breakfast Table,* however. Both DeLancey Ferguson, in 1943, and Bradford A. Booth, in 1950, noted that Clemens used *Autocrat* as a "courting book."[11] Some fifty years later, some of Clemens's marginal annotations begin to fall into a contextual pattern. One of the most notable, in light of Langdon's interests in science, occurs next to the "Autocrat's" pronouncement that "if one's intimate in love or friendship cannot or does not share in all one's intellectual tastes or pursuits, that is a small matter." Here, Clemens crossed out "cannot or," and noted in the margin: "I'm glad of it – because Humor & Phylosophy & Chemistry follow different grooves!" Clearly Clemens was referring to Langdon's interests in chemistry and physics (which Clemens consistently referred to as "Philosophy," dropping the "Natural"), with its valuation of facts and procedures, in contrast to his own interest in the disruptive and exaggerating effects of humor. Similarly, in an aside written next to the Autocrat's lecture on the small number of people who should be invited to share one's intimate thoughts and emotions, Clemens meditated: "I ought not to have said what I did in Wendell Phillips' presence 3 days ago, & which produced a blush which touches me yet with distress – and will for many days to come." Having attended Phillips's lecture at the Elmira Opera House with the Langdons – who were acquainted with Phillips and often shared his views – Clemens had clearly revealed his intimate relationship with Olivia Langdon by some remark spoken in front of the great man and the other company. Langdon's embarrassed response became one of many in Clemens's pantheon of transgressions over which he agonized throughout their lives together. Finally, and in keeping with their discussions about Langdon's reluctance to leave home, Clemens noted next to the Autocrat's meditation on the pain of pulling up roots, "We will plant them again Livy."

As we have seen, the books Langdon sent Clemens often focused on marriage and the roles of husband and wife – subjects that she, as a woman who expected her life's work to consist of marriage and family, would have ranked high on her list of important topics. She, too, "marked" texts, and not always only for edification. At times she even used religious tracts as courtship vehicles. The issues of Henry Ward Beecher's sermons, published weekly as the *Plymouth Pulpit*, and articles from Thomas K. Beecher's *Friday Miscellany* column in the *Advertiser*, were the basis of many of Langdon's and Clemens's discussions. "I am reading the sermon, & I like it," he told her in late August 1869. "I have already read all the places the dainty little fingers marked, & have gone back to start at the beginning" (*MTL* 3: 323). Sometimes she showed her sense of humor in her marks: "*Man is a tease,*" she apparently marked in a sermon of Henry Ward Beecher's early in 1869. "You marked that for *me*, you little rascal," Clemens responded. But he went on to read the entire pamphlet. "You found little in it to mark, but what there was, was Truth, & came home to me" (*MTL* 3: 49). Beecher's sermon – on self-control and self-denial – could have been created with Clemens in mind. As Clemens used the rhetorical strategies at his command to "convert" Langdon to his view of their relationship, so she used her own and her Beecher friends' rhetorics both to show her affections and to convert him to the ideology and practice of Christian manhood.

Langdon and Clemens also discussed political ideas and critiqued writers' styles. In one angry letter, Clemens criticized Thomas K. Beecher, entreating Langdon to see how even her beloved minister could use his rhetorical power for unfair ends. One of Beecher's *Miscellany* columns had attacked Horace Greeley's defense of Freedmen's communities organized for self-help and self-sufficiency. Beecher's attack – one not untypical of him – implied that Greeley was encouraging African Americans to become greedy, selfish, "self-asserting atoms" rather than loving brethren in Christ (*MTL* 3: 155). Clemens responded angrily: "Read this part of the Miscellany again, Livy, & tell me truly if you ever saw a text so misconstrued, so utterly misinterpreted in all your life. ... Mr. Greeley has always argued simply against a poor, unmanly, mean-spirited *dependence* of a man upon his friends for his bread – & behold how Mr. Beecher has distorted his intent" (*MTL* 3: 154). In sending Clemens Beecher's column, Langdon had invited him to discuss her minister's often quirky or even obtuse Christian interpretations of moral behavior; in responding by attacking Beecher's distorting rhetoric, Clemens gave notice that even as a Christian he would maintain his independent judgment about the uses of writing in the social sphere. Exchanges such as this, common enough among the socially conscious Langdons and their friends, suggest that Clemens and Langdon's relationship was in part founded on decided, though friendly, disagreement and debate.

When Clemens first met the Langdon family they considered him a likable but wild and probably unsuitable young man. Twenty-five months later they gave him their daughter, bought and furnished a house for the couple, and lent him a substantial part of the money necessary to buy a one-third share of the Buffalo *Express*. Though their feminist friend Anna Dickinson continued to consider him a boor,[12] the Langdons apparently never regretted having allowed Clemens to "steal" away their "jewel."

The courtship letters document the ways Clemens convinced them that they should welcome him into the fold. Alternately becoming, as he wrote, religious aspirant, prospective son-in-law, businessman, book lover, admirer, preacher, sympathetic brother, and eager lover, Clemens literally *wrote* his way into the Langdon home and into Olivia Langdon's affections. "This, my precious Livy, is the last letter of a correspondence that has lasted seventeen months," he told her on January 20, 1870, just before he stopped lecturing and came to Elmira to prepare for the wedding on February 2. "For over two months of the time, we wrote every other day. During the succeeding twelve months we have written *every* day that we have been parted from each other." Characterizing the correspondence as "the pleasantest . . . I ever had a share in," Clemens thanked her for the "thrill of pleasure" her letters gave him each day and told her that he prayed for her as he had done "since you moved my spirit to prayer seventeen months ago." Introducing one final, elegiac voice, he closed this chapter of their writing lives with cadential finality:

> This is the last long correspondence we ever shall have, my Livy – & now it . . . passes forever from its honored place among our daily occupations, & becomes a *memory*. A memory to be laid reverently away in the holy of holies of our hearts and cherished as a sacred thing. A memory whose momentoes [*sic*] will be precious while we live, and sacred when either one shall die." (*MTL* 4: 31–4)

CONNING BOOKS: OLIVIA LANGDON
AND SAMUEL CLEMENS'S
JOINT READING

The vehemence, if not the explicit language, of Clemens's love letters betrays his fear that his and Langdon's differences were irresolvable. Yet on the surface, at least, they were not: certainly Langdon's parents accepted Clemens's assurances that he really was a changed man, and their own fiscal history predisposed them to look favorably on his material ambitions. Money, morality, and social status were not the problems. Rather, Clemens's fears sprang from his perception of his and Langdon's intellectual and emotional differences, that is, the ways they responded to language, authority, and ideas, especially as these were encoded in the works they read. The immense importance reading played in both their lives enables us to look at their responses to books as a reflection of their overall orientations to life: it is possible to say that each "read" life as he or she read books. As a couple, the compromises – the balancing acts – that they worked out over their disparate responses to what they read is a sign of their ability to, if not resolve differences, at least juggle them, providing each a safe space in which to test her or his more radical ideas. In exploring Langdon's and Clemens's responses to the works they read jointly during the courtship period, we begin to see some of the foundations of their relationship.

Certainly Olivia Langdon and Samuel Clemens were too much a part of their culture not to be enmeshed in the same textual web. For both, history and biography served informational and hagiographical purposes, science began answering fundamental questions about the material world, and fiction was most important as moral instruction. As readers, they were subject to similar textual ploys, as the works they read tried to construct them in the text's own images. Yet here as elsewhere there were sharp differences of both temperament and training. Although books may have made the same demands on them, Langdon and Clemens brought different reading strategies to written materials, resulting in very different reading experiences. This is especially evident in their responses to fiction and to historical works.

As Twain implicitly pointed out in "Some Learned Fables for Good Old Boys and Girls," sublanguages (or specialized languages) create power hierarchies, especially when they are embedded in highly regarded works. Like books about science, literary and historical texts also construct hierarchies of power, both among the characters within them and with the putative readers beyond them. Most readers respond to works of fiction when two or more common axes – that is, axes common to textual characters and the reader – intersect. The texts, in turn, seek to control readers' ideas about personal relationships, to reshape their values, and to reconfigure their sense of the possibilities of wielding power as their culture defines it. Similarly, historical texts also appeal to the familiar and then seek to take their readers into the new. The number of nineteenth-century women readers drawn to biographies of historical women, for instance, testifies to those works' appeal to the familiar (their common gender) and the strange (the fact that, in defiance of cultural norms, the subject of the biography had done something to make her the object of public interest). The ideologies these biographies project, in turn, often seek to control readers' ambitions and ideals. As reconstructions of past events, histories and biographies not only control access to the variegated power struggles of that past but attempt to shape readers' definitions of power itself.

Of course not all readers accept the terms by which they are figured by the texts they read. As Judith Fetterley has demonstrated for women readers of male-oriented works, it is possible to "resist" attempts to shape readers' perceptions.[1] In these cases, an active struggle for power erupts, as readers confront, reject, or reshape (or all three) the ideation the works seek to impose. Certainly this resistance marks Clemens's refusal to confront *Aurora Leigh*'s indictment of male arrogance; similarly, it marks Langdon's refusal to accept Patmore's Honoria as a role model. Personal style, too, comes into play here. Clemens appears as a resisting reader, vehemently responding to the works he read, whereas Langdon approached books very cautiously, "studying out" their meanings rather than hastily responding to them. Additionally, both consciously read as members of social groups rather than as isolated intellects, and both read through their participation in their culture's ongoing debates. In addition to recognizing their individual styles and interests, then, we need to study their cultural contexts – especially, here, the values and expectations widely regarded as marking the differences between men and women. In tandem with personal interests, the gendered contexts of nineteenth-century reading often dictated how readers would process what they read. Like their responses to life in general, Langdon's and Clemens's approaches to books sprang from their differing temperaments, experiences, values, and educations.

One striking example of the differences between Olivia Langdon's and Samuel Clemens's reading behaviors occurs in the records they left of their readings of Charles Dickens's *Dombey and Son*. Like most of Dickens's novels, *Dombey and Son* has two interrelated plots: a story of the Victorian upper-middle class, focused on family relationships and romantic love, and a story of English social types, focused on the marginal and the bizarre. In this novel, the first plot concerns the Dombey family, whose paterfamilias, Mr. Dombey, is powerful, arrogant, and emotionally frigid; the second plot concerns the marginal figures – Solomon Gills, Captain Cuttle, Susan Nipper, and others – who aid and befriend Florence Dombey when she flees her father's cruelty. Both Langdon and Clemens had read *Dombey and Son* before they met: Clemens sometime prior to 1862, Langdon (judging from the proximity of quotations from it to other quotations that are dated) probably in 1865. In his letters Clemens mentioned the text three times. The first occurred in a letter to his mother written from Carson City, Nevada. Describing a recent trip to Humboldt, he listed Dickens's text as one of three books (the others were a copy of Watts's hymns and Lowell Mason's *Carmina Sacra; or, Boston Collection of Church Music*) that accompanied the party (*MTL* 1: 147). Two months later it came crowding into his consciousness as he wrote a friend:

> Oh, no, we won't stuff ballot-boxes and go to congress nor nothing. By no means. "I hope I'm not a oyster though I may not wish to live in crowds." Now I don't mean to say that Nipper's remark is at all pertinent, you know, but I just happened to think of "them old Skettleses," and the quotation followed as a matter of course. And equally of course, the whole Dombey family come trooping after: Cap'en Cuttle, mariner, as Uncle Sol's successor, polishing the chronometers, and making calculations concerning the ebb and flow of the human tide in the street; and watching the stars with a growing interest, as if he felt that he had fallen heir to a certain amount of stock in them; and that old fool of a nurse at Brighton, who thought the house was so "gashly;" and "that Innocent," Toots; and the fat Biler; and Florence, my darling; and "rough old Joey B., Sir;" and "Wal'r, my lad," and the Cap'en's eccentric timepiece, and his sugar tongs, and other little property which he "made over, jintly;" and looming grandly in the rear, comes ponderous Jack Bunsby! Oh, d—n it, I wish I had the book. (*MTL* 1: 166–7)

Clemens referred to *Dombey and Son* periodically in other writings throughout the succeeding half century, usually in reference to the character of Captain Cuttle.[2]

Meanwhile, Olivia Langdon had copied two passages from Dickens's text into her commonplace book. The first also refers to Captain Cuttle; its context is a description of Cuttle in the act of sheltering Florence after she has fled her father's house. Cuttle has put her to bed in Sol Gill's house/shop, and has crept up to check on her. The comparisons of hands refers to Mr. Dombey's hand, which has struck and bruised Florence "on the breast," and Cuttle's "hand," which is actually a hook.

> Long may it remain in this mixed world a point not easy of decision, which is the more beautiful evidence of the Almighty's goodness – the delicate fingers that are formed for sensitiveness and sympathy of touch, and made to minister to pain and grief, or the rough hard Captain Cuttle's hand, that the heart teaches, guides, and softens in a moment![3]

Langdon's second quotation is taken from a section describing the aftermath of Florence's wedding, when she and Walter, her new husband, are setting out on a voyage. They are happily sitting together in the moonlight; Florence is thinking about both Walter and her dead brother, Paul, and the narrator takes over the text to tell us that

> the voices in the waves are always whispering to Florence, in their ceaseless murmuring, of love – of love, eternal and illimitable, not bounded by the confines of this world, or by the end of time, but ranging still, beyond the sea, beyond the sky, to the invisible country far away! (829)

Clemens and Langdon read this text for different ends. Clemens, in 1862 still very much an apprentice writer, was most fascinated by Dickens's comic characters, especially the portrait of Captain Cuttle, who combined comedy and sentiment in wonderfully balanced proportions. Additionally, Clemens was acutely attuned to the extraordinary multiplicity of Dickens's voices, remembering not only the characters but the sublanguages they spoke and the quirks, or tics, that individualized them. Clemens was impressed by Dickens's virtuosity and almost viscerally attracted to the way he typecast his characters.

In contrast, Langdon was interested in the way the author developed family ties, especially the web of relationships between Florence, the heroine, and her male companions – her father, father-surrogate, brother, and lover. Situating herself in the text,

Langdon copied passages that explored the heroine's relationships, the first comparing and contrasting the relationship between Florence's rich but brutal father and her poor and addlepated but kind-hearted protector, the second fusing sexual and fraternal love, oceanic imagery, and the idea of the infinite, Florence's dream of emotional sustenance. Whereas Clemens's reading strategy was professional – he was fascinated by how the characters were constructed – Langdon's was both didactic and exemplary – she studied Cuttle's moral character and Florence's ability to negotiate power and to construct viable relationships.

Clearly these reading strategies reflect Clemens's and Langdon's personal interests and histories. We can also think of them as gendered, seeing Clemens's propensity to study specific characters, isolating them from the context of the plot, as, in psychological terms, symptomatic of male individuation, whereas Langdon's search for relationships is characteristic of the particular empathy of female development.[4] Reared in a culture that saw women almost exclusively in relational terms – as daughters, sisters, wives, or mothers – Langdon approached *Dombey and Son* as a story about a rich girl moving from one to another set of relationships with men. Although this may signal Langdon's female psychology, however, it does not appear to signal a particular interest in women's communities. In fact, Langdon's choice of passages from the novel is notable for its lack of interest in relationships between women. While Dickens's text does foreground Florence's twenty-year process of negotiating alliances with the male characters who shape her life, Florence is also influenced by female characters who try to help her. From the scanty evidence of the passages she copied, Langdon did not seem interested in Florence's women friends, a sign that her reading of *Dombey and Son*, as of works prescribing women's proper roles, was part of her effort to understand the connections between heterosexual love objects, passivity, and power, rather than a strategy to find alternatives to her culture's androcentrism. Clemens's reading strategies, meanwhile, demonstrated other values. Whereas Langdon looked for evidence of relationships, he looked for evidence of uniqueness, even idiosyncrasy. Enculturated by definitions of manhood that stressed the individual, and propelled by his personal penchant for the extreme, Clemens read for characters that stood out from the crowd.

The passages Langdon and Clemens copied or quoted from *Dombey and Son* also indicate where each stood along some of the other strands composing the complex web of Victorian American culture. As an artifact, the result of millions of choices about how to live, cultures articulate a given society's decisions about which aspects of human life it wishes to recognize and, hence, value. Creating binary opposites as they choose cultural values, over time societies also create a substrata of devalued possibilities that are always latently present in high culture and often openly acknowledged in popular media. The literary theorist Mikhail Bakhtin has pointed out that the Feast of Fools was one way medieval church culture contained popular rebellion against its liturgical rigidity by tolerating parodic episodes.[5] Similarly, nineteenth-century American culture vented its rigid behavioral codes during regularly appointed carnivals such as election days and revivals. If we examine culturally devalued possibilities on this social level, we see them manifesting themselves as group desires, quasi-obsessive fascinations with the forbidden. Nineteenth-century temperance tracts, for instance, with the traces of temperance themes found in other forms of contemporary literature, were as much signs of the mixture of fear and curiosity inspired by inebriation – seen as loss of control – as they were signs of the pervasiveness of American alcoholism. On an individual level, on the other hand, culturally devalued possibilities appear, paradoxically, in their absences, that is, as desire, as movement toward the forbidden or the unknown. Sometimes filled by figural substitutions (as, in a Freudian sense, of religious for sexual desire), these gaps signal the inarticulable and, at times, the unthinkable.

The most striking set of cultural values evident in the writings – private and public, original or quoted – of Olivia Langdon and Samuel Clemens hovers around the issues of duty and control. Central to any discussion of Victorian mores, control, or lack of it, is also a recurring topic in discussions both of Clemens's personality and of his relationship with his wife (where she has usually been projected as controlling him). Langdon's own struggles over the issues of duty and control have been generally ignored. But as we have already seen from selections in her commonplace book, her careful construction of a litany of inspirational texts on learning self-control and performing duty demonstrates how seriously she took these issues. By the same token, the number of entries acknowledging the need for self-control, especially as self-abnegation, and the importance of duty, also suggest that she felt inadequate on both scores. Far from preparation for domination, Langdon's search suggests that she was trying to subordinate her own desires to her perception of what other people wanted of her. On her twenty-second birthday, for instance, she told Alice Hooker that

> if I only grow in Grace and in the knowledge of our Lord and Saviour [*sic*] I am content. . . . You may know how with all the tokens of affection from friends is renewed the desire to be to them all I can, to cultivate day by day all the powers that are given me, that will be of pleasure or service to them – Yet I feel more and more keenly, that of my Self I am utterly incompetent to do *any thing*. But I hope that I am learning more and more where to look for strength. (November 28, 1867, Stowe-Day)

Though much here approaches the clichés of traditional piety, there is also, as there had been in her mother's prayer for family grace on her own birthday a year earlier (August 19, 1866), a genuine hope that divine intercession would facilitate selflessness.

On one level, this, too, is a gendered agenda; the image of the good woman in nineteenth-century culture stressed abnegation, and women's prayers for strength to rid themselves of self are hallmarks of their private writings. Additionally, Langdon knew that her long illness had created anxieties and troubles for her family that left her deeply in their debt. But Langdon's focus on duty and control also suggests that she was aware of the potential for disorder and chaos in a very real sense, and was searching for ways to counteract it. One of her quotations from *The Marble Faun* suggests as much: in this passage Hawthorne's narrator is celebrating the fact that all women sew, and comments that "they have greatly the advantage of us [men] in this respect. The slender thread of silk or cotton keeps them united with the small, familiar, gentle interests of life, the continually operating influences of which do so much for the health of the character, and carry off what would otherwise be a dangerous accumulation of morbid sensibility."[6] Like exercise, sewing is projected here as a means to withstand "morbidity," or depression, through repeated physical activity. Additionally, for Hawthorne sewing created community among women: "A vast deal of human sympathy runs along this electric line, stretching from the throne to the wicker-chair of the humblest seamstress, and keeping high and low in a species of communion with their kindred beings" (*Marble Faun*, 40). Here, community and mental stability are figured as interlocking effects of a common gendered activity that is posited in contrast to a male sphere implicitly characterized by lack of community and mental instability.

On a personal level, Langdon's sensitivity to the possibilities of disorder might have been a result of her years confined to bed, constantly aware of the destabilizing potential of tedium and pain. Certainly the discipline she had learned there endured, becoming part of the value system she brought to her evaluation of other people's complaints. Many years later, for instance, she noted in her diary,

> I am reading with great interest "George Eliot's Life" by her husband J. W. Cross. It is most delightful – you live with her in a most real way – the only thing in the book that annoys me is her constant mention of her ill health. How can a woman that was so great as she, be so interested and absorbed in how she feels, how her headache is, that she always mentions the fact in her journal and in her letters. It seems as if [such] remarks should have been left out in the editing. The only thing that would seem to excuse their being left in, is that they

show how much a person may accomplish with great physical inability and much mental depression. At any rate the "Life" carries you on giving you strong impressions of all her moods and struggles in a most marvelous way.[7]

Here Langdon's sense of self-control, her belief that one does not impose one's own physical disabilities on others, combined with her sense of decorum and, by 1885, her knowledge of editing, provide one set of criteria through which she read.

Langdon's sensitivity to disorder may also have been related to her observations of the chaos that lay beneath the genteel rationality of Victorian culture, from the Civil War and its aftermath to the record of fires, rapes, drunkenness, murder, and other mayhem constantly reported in the daily papers, including Elmira's *Advertiser*. Despite her status as the daughter of one of the wealthiest men in town, and her personal history of confinement in sanitariums and other therapeutic residences, Langdon was not isolated from her society's problems and was well able to judge the temper of the times from second- if not firsthand experience. For instance, between 1866 and 1870, when she was spending most of her time at home, both local and national papers were full of news about the Fenians, a secret group of Irish revolutionaries set on overturning English rule, whose branches in the United States brought the possibilities of terrorism close to home.[8] Irish immigrants of all classes had been prominent in the Elmira area since the American Revolution, and by the 1860s the proportion of Irish was large enough to make reporting of Irish news a lucrative activity for local papers.[9] The passions and the dangers of the Fenians' quarrels were reported with such frequency that Olivia Lewis kept track of them, noting at one point, for instance, that "the news is quite startling in regard to the Fenians. They are likely to make much trouble on the Canadian frontier" (OLL Diary, June 4, 1866). Similarly, news of America's freedmen and the society's tumultuous race relations were regularly reported by the staunchly Republican *Advertiser* and discussed by the Langdon family. And of course local crimes were

faithfully reported. The *Advertiser*'s summary of Chemung County's prison commitments for the year 1865 included 429 for
drunkenness and disorderly conduct, 127 for prostitution, 94 for
petty larceny, 53 for grand larceny, 45 for assault and battery, 14
for murder, 9 for burglary and 1 for rape.[10] On January 31, 1867,
the paper's lead article concerned a man who had just whipped
his three-year-old child to death; the *Saturday Evening Review* in
1869 did not shrink from reporting controversies over the legality
of abortion,[11] and a series of mysterious fires motivated Olivia
Lewis to record that "March of 1866 will long be remembered
as the month in which there occurred in Elmira 23 fires, most of
them the work of incendiaries. I have suffered a great deal from
fearful apprehensions in regard to it" (OLL Diary, April 3, 1866).
The spectacle of a society in the process of destroying itself
loomed as ominously in Elmira as in the metropolis, and the need
for self-control, on both personal and public levels, was a corollary
often voiced from pulpits and from editors' chairs. Olivia Langdon's collection of quotations focusing on the achievement of
control, then, is not surprising. Both as a suggestion of her construction of self, and as sign of her interest in the relationship
between civilization and restraint, these documents help us place
her along one continuum that could be labeled "duty–desire,"
where "desire" stands for her perception of her own or others'
wills to recognize their personal imperatives to their own satisfaction, and "duty" stands for her own and others' wills to emphasize communal needs. Her shuttles along this continuum are one
of the shaping elements of her life.

   In contrast to Langdon's continuum, which demands that subjects choose one set of cultural values over another, Clemens participated in two spheres at once. Enculturated in and espousing
mainstream values, he nevertheless dwelt, in his artistic life if not
in his personal one, in a zone we can call "wild," where "wildness" stands for the will to adventure beyond the boundaries of
the community, which for him stood for the known, the safe, and
the culturally acceptable. As countless observers have remarked,
Clemens courted propriety (usually envisioned as Langdon and

the Elmira/Hartford circle) as a backdrop to his frequent demonstrations of impropriety. Apparently happy to live on the margins of the official culture (which clung to its sense of order in the face of the profound incivility of postbellum culture), Clemens nevertheless badly needed its strictures to construct his rebellions, and his dualism was one of his most notable characteristics. But he was also acutely attuned to the muted structures of his society, those elements of life that official culture did not recognize. With his ear for the sublanguages or specialized languages – the heteroglossia – around him, this sensitivity was the basis of much of his humor and also of many of his excesses – his proclivity to give voice to aspects of his culture that had been relegated to the realm of the popular, and in some instances had even become the forbidden. It was also one of the bases for his explorations into the possibility of alternative realities and his fascination with psychological aberrations.[12]

Even during these relatively early years Clemens's writing showed signs of his experiments in exploring what it felt like to be the "Other," especially the forbidden Other, rather than disavowing it. As a humorist, especially of the western stamp, he was of course not held to ordinary rules of literary decorum, and his burlesques of forms ("A New Biography of George Washington," "The Revised Catechism") show his resistance to formal hagiography, while his early attacks on white Americans' cruelty to Chinese immigrants ("Goldsmith's Friend Abroad Again") show the oppositional anger that would later stimulate his own Swiftean prose. Most pertinent here, however, are two pieces from 1876, "The Facts Concerning the Recent Carnival of Crime in Connecticut" and "[Date 1601] Conversation, as it Was by the Social Fireside, in the Time of the Tudors." Both are experiments in articulating the subject positions – the socially constructed points of view – of muted (here, forbidden) elements of the Victorian psyche.

As all readers recognize, "The Facts Concerning the Recent Carnival of Crime in Connecticut" is a fantasy about losing self-control. Confronted by the fleshly manifestation of his con-

(*top*) Elmira, New York *c.* 1873. The Chemung County Historical Society, Elmira, New York.

(*bottom*) Elmira, New York, Lake St., *c.* 1868. The Chemung County Historical Society, Elmira, New York.

science, "a vague, general, evenly-blended, nicely-adjusted de-
formity . . . covered all over with a fuzzy greenish mold, such as
one sometimes sees upon mildewed bread,"[13] the first-person narrator flies into "a blind rage" (649), accuses it of having "dogged, and dogged, and *dogged* me, all the days of my life" (652),
and finally kills it. The act of violence delights him: "In an instant
I had my life-long foe by the throat . . . I tore him to shreds and
fragments. I rent the fragments into bits. I cast the bleeding fragments into the fire, and drew into my nostrils the grateful incense
of my burnt-offering. At last, and forever, my Conscience was
dead!" (659). Now "a free man!" he rampages throughout the
countryside, killing his enemies, burning a house that obstructs
his view, robbing and swindling and generally having a good time.

Thematically, the story is all about satisfying personal desire;
what is remarkable – and shocking – about it is the intense nar-
ratorial pleasure it conveys.[14] The title (Twain has many titles beginning "The Facts Concerning") suggests that it is to be a piece
of investigative journalism; in fact, it is a revelation of the energy
of an unguarded id that not only thematically but rhythmically
crescendos in an exultant cry of freedom: "You behold before
you a man whose life-conflict is done, whose soul is at peace; a
man whose heart is dead to sorrow, dead to suffering, dead to
remorse; a man WITHOUT A CONSCIENCE!" (659–60). Written from beyond Victorian boundaries, this story fuses language
and theme to illustrate Twain's ventures into a realm in which
the literary contemplation of untrammeled desire renders personal "bliss, unalloyed bliss" (660). It is not surprising that
"Facts" was first presented to the all-male Monday Evening Club,
which met in the well-appointed parlors of the Hartford literati
and relegated women to the marginal spaces of the house. Like
"1601," "Facts Concerning" works best within the context of
repression and rebellion in which it was produced.

"[Date 1601] Conversation, as it Was by the Social Fireside, in
the Time of the Tudors," also explores the forbidden. Certainly
one way to look at "1601" is as one of Twain's attempts to radically disrupt the fabric of nineteenth-century life by affronting

his contemporaries. Here he fused the names of well-known historical personages – the figures Langdon and her friends had been taught to recognize – and the vocabulary and syntax of a historical language that readers of Sidney and Shakespeare had been taught to revere, with references to bodily functions that all his readers knew were *verboten*. Viewed from within the culture, "1601" is a work calculated to outrage the educated bourgeois.[15]

A more fruitful way to look at "1601," however, is as a putative exercise in reconstructing sixteenth-century English that takes advantage of Elizabethan customs to circumvent nineteenth-century mores. Perhaps Clemens had read, or heard about, Thomas Nashe's "Choice of Valentines" or other pornographic sixteenth-century works; his reference to Margrette of Navarre, who wrote sixteenth-century erotica, suggests that he had. Certainly he was familiar with contemporary pornography. But "1601" does not titillate, it embarrasses. Like the ending of "Facts," this piece can result in social chaos; the difference, of course, is that the chaos here lies not within the story's parameters but without, in the conflicted emotions of readers who find themselves laughing and blushing at the same time.

With his delight in multiple voices that fused ideologies with linguistic modes, Twain was fascinated by the degree to which some sublanguages permitted the voicing of what was to his culture impermissible. "1601" illustrates this fascination through two subjects unspeakable in the nineteenth century: first, it foregrounds farting, not only featuring characters who accuse each other of having farted, but also describing those farts. Second, it discusses sex. It has long been regarded as Mark Twain's "Other" writing, the clandestine piece that demonstrates the prurience in the midst of his professions of propriety. To see it this way, though, is to assume that Twain was writing from within the mainstream rather than from a sphere in which farts and erections were acceptable topics of conversation. As he burlesqued the "language" of scientific adepts and attacked its practitioners for their arrogance in "A Fable for Good Old Boys and Girls," in "1601" Twain voiced the unspeakable, writing of a time "when pricks were stiff and cunts not loath to take ye stiffness out of them,"[16] and of having Queen Elizabeth declare that "in mine eight and sixty yeres have I not heard the fellow to this fart" (660). Conscious that he was writing in a tradition, Twain also repeated Boccaccio, having "Sr W" (Sir Walter Raleigh) entertain the company with a story

> of a priest that did beguile a maid into his cell, then knelt him in a corner to pray for grace to be rightly thankful for this tender maidenhead ye Lord had sent him; but ye abbot, spying through ye key-hole, did see a tuft of brownish hair with fair white flesh about it, wherefore when ye priest's prayer was done his chance was gone, forasmuch as ye little maid had but ye one cunt, and that was already occupied to her content. (665)

It is interesting that Twain, like writers of the sixteenth century, gave equal weight to female and male sexual desire, having "Master Shaxpur" speak of "an empress" who "did entertain two and twenty lusty knights between her sheetes, yet was not satisfied" (664), and attributing forthright expressions of sexual interest to the company's women, old and young.[17] What little resistance arises to the characters' conversation is relegated to the voice of an ancient, prissy narrator, but this voice is, in effect, canceled by the forthright cheerfulness of the principals. Comfortably situated in their own territory, Twain's principal characters converse unself-consciously. In fact, the characters' lack of self-consciousness is precisely where "1601" differs from traditional pornography; for the dominant impression the piece conveys is the author's delight in constructing the characters' worldviews. Rather than being written to stimulate jaded appetites or shock the bourgeoisie, the primary intent of "1601" is to speak from a location where bodily functions are both central and celebrated.

Whereas Langdon's strong sense of duty and control led her to value the community and to work to perfect its possibilities, then, Clemens's dual vision led him to explore the subjectivity of the Other. We can return to *Dombey and Son* as an example of some of the ways these systems operated in Langdon's and Clemens's reading perceptions. Though they chose to focus on vastly different aspects of the novel, both readers emphasized Captain Cuttle. Langdon, however, chose to record Cuttle in his most contained, most dutiful moment – when he, already having assumed responsibility for his absent friend's shop, aided and sustained Florence in her hour of need. Responsibility – surrogate fatherhood – tempers his oddness and brings him, at least temporarily, into the world of the ordinary; his flightiness, his generous but undisciplined sensibility, is educated and contained by his new responsibilities. For Langdon, Cuttle was most valuable after he had assumed mainstream manners, not because his oddity itself offended her, but because he had subordinated his own desires to the needs of others, thus creating a new community from the disorder into which the Dombey house had fallen.

Clemens, on the other hand, remembered Cuttle in all his oddity, his fixation on the value of his silver sugar tongs and his out-of-sync watch, his discombobulated talk and his rapid walk, his curiosity about mankind and his calculations of the stars. Dickens's comic characters are remarkable for the way they negotiate madness, remaining within the boundaries of the acceptable while constantly threatening to break out of it. In addition to his professional interest in how Dickens developed them, Clemens was also attracted to these characters because they came so close to breaking the tethers that held them, always tenuously, to the Victorian norm. Like the bizarre characters populating western and southwestern fiction, Dickens's comic characters hovered on the margins of the mainstream and articulated worldviews existing, at best, tangentially to commonly held assumptions. Whereas Langdon sought to remember how duty, expressed in relational terms, tamed and contained marginal characters, Clemens wanted to discover how far comic characters could stray beyond the pale before they became sketches of madness rather than parodies of class behaviors.

The record left by Langdon and Clemens of their reactions to *The Merchant of Venice* suggests similar responses. Here Langdon, drawn to the centers of power, was attracted to the controlling figure of the play, whereas Clemens, reading from beyond the mentality that enshrines the Bard, parodied Shakespeare's language and referred most often to the character who tried to disrupt the self-satisfied flow of Venetian life. In her commonplace book Langdon quoted three passages from *The Merchant of Venice*, all Portia's speeches. All are famous; as noted earlier, a major function played by Langdon's Shakespeare studies was to familiarize her with some of her culture's most valuable cultural commodities. Her choice to record Portia's lines exclusively, however, was dictated as much by gender interests as by cultural prerogatives. From a gynocritical point of view, the interesting fact about this play is that even though Portia voluntarily subordinates herself to Bassanio she still controls the course of events. Two of the passages Langdon copied are from act 3, scene 2: in the first Portia greets Bassanio, confesses her love for him, and suggests that she can teach him how to pass the test that will win her hand; in the second she places "this house, these servants and this same myself" at his service (act 3, scene 2, line 172). Even in a marriage game in which she has begun by lamenting her own powerlessness, Portia finds ways to ensure that the man who wins her is the one she has chosen. The third passage Langdon copied is Portia's plea for mercy to Shylock. Here the "unschooled" woman, freed from the need to make verbal professions of inferiority by masquerading as a man, demonstrates her extraordinary intelligence, eloquence, and knowledge of the law. Perhaps most important, she halts an apparently remorseless process that in its cannibalistic vengefulness promises to destroy the fabric of Venetian life. In confronting and vanquishing Shylock, Portia is the hero who stays the onset of anarchy and chaos.

Read through the themes foregrounded in Langdon's letters and in the construction of her commonplace book, Portia becomes a powerful figure who can fuse desire with duty (her desire for Bassanio with her duty to obey her father's memory), swear subordination to her husband, save her husband's honor and the life of his friend, and preserve the fabric of Venetian life. In her search for a way to continue exploring her own potential for self-creation while conforming to her society's gender expectations, Langdon, as other women, may well have found Portia a powerful – and ultimately subversive – role model.[18]

Not at all interested in the feminist aspects of the play, in the course of his writing life Clemens quotes – but changes – Portia's "mercy" speech twice, refers to a minor passage of Gratiano's once, uses Shylock as a metonym for merciless greed several times and, once, quotes Shylock's declaration of his own humanity. As Sander Gilman has recently suggested, Mark Twain's figuring of Shylock in his written work was typical of a culture in which the Jewish body (and this includes the Jewish mentality) represented disease and inspired fear.[19] When in *The Innocents Abroad*, written while he was courting Langdon, Twain refers to "Shylocks in gaberdine and sandals, venturing loans upon the rich argosies of Venetian commerce,"[20] he is reproducing – perhaps pandering to – the cultural image of usurious Jews. Whether his references to Shylock are positive or negative, however, is less pertinent here than that he mentions Shylock more than he mentions any other character in *The Merchant of Venice*. The pariah of Venetian – for Shakespeare and his contemporaries, of Christian – society, Shylock's revenge, if effected, would unhinge Venetian society. Rejecting "mercy," that linchpin of ideal Western morality, Shylock, for all his insistence on the rule of law, is from the Christian point of view a deviant, even a madman, a figure living outside the moral and behavioral norm. As such, he was of great interest to Clemens. Although it was unlikely that Clemens would have publicly defended Shylock, if we read *The Merchant of Venice* through his penchant for otherness, his willingness to dwell psychologically in his culture's wild zone and to explore its forbidden and/ or muted aspects, we can see the fascination Shylock could hold. Mark Twain's tricksters – traditionally, characters who not only dwell beyond their cultures' boundaries but also delight in destroying them – are also relevant here. For a professional reader and creator of trickster tales, Shylock is less mad than a brilliant, if foiled, trickster.

In these early years Clemens also disrupted Portia's famous

speech, putting it in the mouth of a speaker whose style he was also parodying: "Ah, sir, the quality of mercy is not strained, so to speak (as has been aptly suggested heretofore), but droppeth like the gentle dew from Heaven, as it were."[21] Although he would later use another, gentler, passage as an epigraph to *The Prince and the Pauper* (1882), Clemens's confidence that he could remake Shakespeare's language to suit his own needs indicates his less than total reverence for the words of the master. As with other literary comedians who specialized in parodying cultural icons, Twain's parody reveals a desire to disrupt, to destroy, the verbal fabric that expresses his culture's best image of itself.

While Clemens positioned himself within the sensibility of the Other, then, Langdon attempted to minimize the threat of the Other by bringing it within the compound. Her efforts to familiarize the alien were certainly the basis of much scholarly misunderstanding about her relationship with Clemens; those efforts may also, however, be one basis for their close marriage. As I noted earlier, it has long been common to observe that Langdon "controlled" Clemens. On the most simplistic level, this has been a way to blame a wealthy woman for her *auslander* husband's failures. More sophisticated observers have noted that Clemens openly courted Langdon's disapproval, and that he often fabricated it as a comic device in letters, when in fact Langdon was innocent of any attempt at censure. In these instances, Clemens constructed Langdon as his superego, inscribing this character in his letters to friends and thus, probably unwittingly, making the historical Langdon prey to later generations of critical misogynists. A careful reading of Langdon's letters and her commonplace book, however, suggests that a fruitful means of investigation into their intellectual and emotional relationships would be through the assumption that both were acutely, even terribly, aware that wildness – for Langdon, often envisioned as chaos – existed. Attracted by this shared perception, their responses to it differed in that Langdon, working in oppositional terms, attempted to master and to control it, hoping that outward forms would transform the unknown into the known; whereas

126

Clemens played with it, immersing himself in its manifestations and exploring its possibilities. Another quotation in her commonplace book, from Hawthorne's *Marble Faun*, illustrates Langdon's concern for boundaries: "This perception of an infinite, shivering solitude, amid which we cannot come close enough to human beings to be warmed by them, and where they turn to cold, chilly shapes of mist, is one of the most forlorn results of any accident, misfortune, crime, or peculiarity of character, that puts an individual ajar with the world" (*Marble Faun*, 110). Here Hawthorne's narrator, true to his author's obsessions, posits ostracism from the human community as the result of deviant behavior. Langdon, for whom human relationships were the focal point of existence, copied this as a cautionary passage. In contrast, Clemens had a lifelong fascination with just such marginal characters, as is evident in his many mysterious strangers, who in fact dwell in what Hawthorne and Langdon would regard as "an infinite shivering solitude," and who explicitly reject the warmth of other human beings.

Langdon and Clemens, then, shared a vision acutely sensitive to the possibilities of disorder, but they responded to their perceptions in very different ways. Langdon, working from within the mainstream, always sought to create order by building communities; Clemens, often situating himself beyond the boundaries, sought to voice the muted. With this, the forms of control each exhibited were markedly different. In her friendships as in her reading, Langdon searched for examples of people who could sustain conventional relationships (as Portia with Bassanio) while in fact holding real power. In domestic terms, many women, especially among the leisured classes, have always done this, and Olivia Lewis, Langdon's mother, presented an immediate role model. But other older friends also presented interesting examples. Rachel Gleason, for instance, had at least as much power as her husband in running the Elmira Water Cure, and the articles that she published gave her a national reputation. Julia Beecher's influence on the female members of Thomas's congregation was at least as profound as her husband's. Isabella Hooker, both for herself and as a sister to Harriet Beecher Stowe and Catharine Beecher, was an example of a woman who could maintain conventional roles while radically affecting the public sphere. And Anna Dickinson, friend to both Olivia Langdon and her mother, was a widely known public figure whose courage was acknowledged even by those who attacked her views. Though Langdon's married life was far more like her mother's than like the lives of these friends, her willingness to entertain new ideas and her sense that effective power is more a matter of relational dynamics than of outward show is attributable, at least in part, to their influence.

Power is not only dependent on relationships, however. Knowledge – the intellectual constructs a culture develops to understand itself – also yields power. As we have already seen, Langdon sought literary and other information (such as science) that would help her understand her environment historically, politically, and materially. Luise Mühlbach's series of historical fiction on the reign of Frederick the Great is only one of many histories, nonfiction or fictionalized, that Langdon read. Interestingly, Mühlbach's work emphasizes self-control and duty. *Berlin and San Souci or, Frederick the Great and His Friends,* from which Langdon quoted in her commonplace book, focuses both on Frederick's stern self-denial for his country's sake and on his insistence that his family similarly deny themselves. The full context of the passage Langdon copied is part of Frederick's rebuke to his sister Amelia, when she begs him not to force her to marry the king of Denmark:

> "He only is faithful to himself who lives to discharge his duties," said the king. "He only is true to himself who governs himself, and if he cannot be happy, at least endeavors to make others so, and this vocation of making others happy is the noblest calling for a woman; by this shall she overcome her selfishness and find comfort, strength, and peace."[22]

Despite the king's fine words, in Mühlbach's text Amelia does not obey her brother; rather, she disfigures herself so that she will no longer be marriageable. At once admiring of Frederick's self-abnegation and critical of his effects on others, Mühlbach's work records recent German history while raising serious questions about the nature of authoritarian relationships. Similarly, John Motley's three-volume *Rise of the Dutch Republic*, the last volume of which Langdon told Hooker she was reading, focuses on Holland's political and religious history, especially William of Orange's struggles against the absolutism of Philip II. Here, too, the author scrutinizes major characters for their moral integrity, leadership qualities, attention to duty, and self-control. Armed with unquestioned assumptions about the qualities that make for greatness, nineteenth-century writers of history – whether fictionalized or not – continually articulated their criteria and judged their characters accordingly. The most didactic aspects of their texts consist of their promulgation of values that play only limited variations on the themes of duty and self-control. In addition to its work of enculturating her as a member of a class that expressed its power through displays of knowledge as well as of wealth, then, Langdon's reading in history and literature helped her construct a variety of overlapping strategies for controlling self and world. On both psychological and social levels, Langdon's sense of the possibilities of power was educated by the many biographies and histories that her contemporaries wrote, in part, to teach their readers how to live.

Clemens's relationship to power and control was more complicated. Always a psychological parvenu, his most evident form of control over others expressed itself in trickster terms, and the trickster element in his writing expresses one aspect of his relationship to mainstream values and constructions of reality.

Additionally, as a reader, Clemens often resisted the authority of other authors' voices. Like Langdon, he read for information; unlike her, he often absorbed authoritative texts' information only to challenge their assumptions, leaving a record of letters, diary entries, and marginalia that suggest, at the very least, his often-intense frustration with the texts' hierarchies of value. Of Motley's work, for instance, he asserted that "it did make me so cordially despise those pitiful Dutchmen and their execrable Republic,"[23] which was certainly not Motley's intent. *The Marble Faun*, which Langdon treated as a guide to wisdom, could, Clemens suggested, be as easily thought "tiresome."[24] Reading Langdon's copy of Carlyle's *French Revolution*, probably in 1870,[25] Clemens sneered at Carlyle's prediction that the people's cries would be "heard in Heaven. And the answer too will come, -in a horror of great darkness, and shakings of the world, and a cup of trembling which all the nations shall drink."[26] To this Clemens responded, in the margin, "Yes, after a thousand years. Let us sing praises, for wonderful promptness, O Providential Show-Coach!"[27] Resisting Carlyle's rhetorical equation of the French Revolution with Armageddon, Clemens read this text as a record of human barbarity. *The French Revolution*'s presence is palpable in much of Clemens's later writing; his admiration for it, however, resulted less from its analysis of causes and personalities than from its confirmation of his own latent misanthropy.

Clemens's resistance to the authority of other writers' voices also explains his lack of sympathy for many of the works that Langdon copied into her commonplace book. Often, he treated these as simply incomprehensible. Humorously volunteering to write a memorial to Langdon's sister, Susan Crane, when the time came, for instance, Clemens told her that in addition to testimonials from heads of state "I'll have some poetry in – some of those sublime conundrums from Young's Night Thoughts which only Livy can . . . cipher out the meaning of, & some dark & bloody mystery out of the Widow Browning – & . . . also some poetry of my own . . . & between the three I guess we'll 'hive' the gentle reader" (May 17 and 18, 1869, *MTL* 3: 241). Here he avoided confronting the reasons he did not like either *Night Thoughts* or *Aurora Leigh*, two of Langdon's favorite works. Certainly one reason was that both were epic poems demanding the kind of close reading that did not interest him. Another was that each advocates positions alien to Clemens at that time of his life: *Night Thoughts* that one examine one's life in view of impending death, *Aurora Leigh* that women have the right to professional independence and self-determination. Perhaps most important, both works assume an air of justified authority that would have irritated Clemens even if he had been sympathetic to their causes. Like many of Langdon's other "inspirational" readings, these works proselytize a particular point of view, explicitly telling readers how to live. The advice that Langdon embraced, recording passages that would inspire her to create an energetic and useful life, Clemens rejected because he didn't like anyone telling him what to do.[28]

With this, Clemens rejected the rhetorical construction of authority such texts contain. As in "Some Fables for Good Old Boys and Girls," pieces that he wrote during these early years parody the sublanguages through which interest groups seek to gain power by undermining those groups' own subject positions. One of the reasons the epistolary document, "Female Suffrage," published in the St. Louis *Missouri Democrat* between March 12 and 15, 1867, strikes many contemporary readers unpleasantly is that Twain constructed his characters' arguments so that they reveal the characters' self-interest rather than debating the question of citizenship. Of the four voices speaking through a putative editorial page, none speaks with any real concern for the process of governance; rather, each uses language to appropriate "turf." Here we see an example of Twain's experiments in constructing and deconstructing multiple subject positions without a core ideology against which he could contrast them.

During the course of the piece "Mark Twain," the "editor" and only male voice, begins by arguing that women should stay out of the electoral process, first because they will greatly expand the number of paid offices, and second because their absence from home while imitating men will force men to take over household duties. "Every man, I take it, has a selfish end in view when he pours out eloquence in behalf of the public good in the newspapers," this speaker admits, "and such is the case with me. ... If you give the women full sweep with the men in political affairs, she will proceed to run for every confounded office ... she would not have time to do anything at all then." [29]

This satire of the male position assumes that men oppose female suffrage out of self-interest. The three female voices that respond to "Mark Twain" are no less self-aggrandizing, however. The first is "Mrs. Mark Twain," who characterizes her husband as a "flippant ass" and his letter as "vile, witless dribblings" (216). The second is a termagant who calls "Mark Twain" an "atrocious scoundrel" and violently asserts that "we will have our rights, though the heavens fall" (217). The third is an otherworldly old maid who seems to be writing because she feels that her years of missionary work entitle her to the vote. To each of these "Mark Twain," taking advantage, apparently, of his editorial power, appends a vindictively destructive rebuttal. Finally, he returns to center stage with a full letter to a "cousin Jennie." Here, he announces that he will "drop the foolishness, and speak with the gravity the occasion demands" because she herself has taken the issue seriously (219–20). First, in good rhetorical style, he makes a strong prosuffrage argument. He concludes, however, with a 180–degree turn, arguing against female suffrage because it would soil the image of the feminine and "reduce" women "to a level with negroes and men" (221). Following this passage of calculated sentimentality and deliberately racist sex-baiting, the writer reverts to the satiric mode in which he had begun four days earlier, claiming that women would never vote because they would have to tell their ages at the polls, that they would pass laws against smoking, infidelity, and so forth. "Women, go your ways!" he concludes. "Seek not to beguile us of our imperial privileges" (220). Finally, postscripting his own letter, "Mark Twain" suggests that his wife is an alcoholic and reveals that he is planning "to touch off a keg of powder" under the suffrage meeting she has scheduled for that night. From verbal to physical violence, this speaker controls and destroys all his opponents.

Both the frustration and the interest of this piece stem from the fact that none of the speakers has a viable position. Clearly, Twain's point is that this battle, like most others, is being fought over questions of self-interest rather than questions of female competence or the conduct of democratic governance. Here, like Dickens, Twain orchestrates the voices of his community in such a way that the ideologies behind their stances come clear; the resulting spectacle reveals a nearly universal mean-mindedness. In the end, none of the positions merits support. More interested in deconstructing textual authorities than in exploring the issue of female suffrage, Twain's satire, unlike Dickens's, destroys one set of positions without suggesting viable alternatives.

As this example demonstrates, part of Twain's genius consisted in moving from one subject position to another, experimenting not only with various points of view but also with those subjects' experiences of others. Often, this also involves deconstructing *other* subject positions: the root of many of Twain's parodies lay in his taking on opponents as he changed point of view. With his constructions of otherness, that is, Twain also destabilized counterideologies. Articulating voices from the wild, he was always ready to become a trickster, to attack mainstream assumptions from the outside. And although it is almost impossible to escape his constant awareness of the Other, the remarkable fact is that unlike other polemicists he struggled to avoid definition.[30]

One final example of Clemens's propensity to resist authorial assumptions reveals neither his deconstructive nor his wild modes, but his very conservative one. Langdon's and Clemens's responses to Thackeray's essay on Swift in *English Humorists* shows Clemens in a mood of violent propriety and Langdon in one of easy acceptance. Two passages from the essay appear in Langdon's commonplace book. In the first, Thackeray, attempting to construct a Swift that nineteenth-century readers could tolerate, celebrates Swift's religious feeling: "Through the storms and tempests of his furious mind, the stars of religion and love break out in the blue, shining serenely, though hidden by the driving clouds and the maddened hurricane of life."[31] In the second, Thackeray tries to explore the sources of Swift's anger, positing that his misanthropy came from his sense of his own worthlessness: "We view the world with our own eyes, each of us; and we make from within us the world we see. A weary heart gets no gladness out of sunshine; a selfish man is skeptical about friendship, as a man with no ear doesn't care for music" (163). For Thackeray, the essay on Swift was a way to negotiate the sensibilities of the eighteenth and nineteenth centuries. For Langdon, the passages she copied, recontextualized in her commonplace book, became inspirations for creating a stable self and an affirmation of personal potential. For Clemens, however, Swift's indecencies provided an insurmountable barrier to appreciation. Resisting Thackeray's text, he copiously annotated its margins, castigating Swift as "a hideous character," with taste "as prurient . . . as Rabelais," and possessed of "mere *intellectual* greatness."[32] Rejecting Thackeray's authorial power to reconstruct his subject, Clemens combined Thackeray's information about Swift with his own sense of literary propriety and denied the validity of the biographer's values. Whereas Langdon was willing to see beyond Swift's lack of control, Clemens refused to transcend its specter.

Gender, class, and personality shaped the differences between Olivia Langdon and Samuel Clemens as readers, as they shaped them in most other spheres. Nevertheless, their common culture, especially as that culture anticipated its own dissolution, moved them to a shared concern with issues of duty and control. Responding differently to texts that masked as authorities, Langdon and Clemens also complemented each other, alternately anchoring while the other wandered. When Langdon normalized, Clemens risked the wild; when Langdon entertained the venomous or the obscene, Clemens raised conventional standards. For us, such cases suggest ways that nineteenth-century readers negotiated relationships between self and other, self and world. Most important, perhaps, they demonstrate how Olivia Langdon and Samuel Clemens created a viable marriage out of a host of apparent dissimilarities. In their responses to texts, as in their responses to much of the rest of the world, we perceive a continuous and bilateral juggling of intellect and emotion that may well have been one of the cementing activities of their relationship.

5

MARRIAGE

I believe that two people who are to unite their lives should feel as sanguine about their future, as you feel about ours. . . . I cannot understand, their chief aim in life being . . . a Christian walk and conversation, knowing the uncertainty of human effort . . . how it can be otherwise, than that they shall help and strengthen each other.

OLC to Mary Fairbanks, January 15, 1869, MTM

I would like to have you or Sue here, I get a little homesick to see you once in a while, tonight I should like to put my head in your lap and cry just a little bit. I want to be somebody's baby – I have two babies, have four servants to manage, I have a glorious husband to try and be a woman for, but sometimes I would like to lie down and give it all up – I feel so incompetent for everything, I come so very far short, yet I think I do try earnestly every day.

OLC to OLL, January 19, 1872, MTM.

When Olivia Langdon wrote the first letter quoted above to Mary Fairbanks in 1869, she was living contentedly at home, her wedding day still vaguely and reassuringly distant. When she wrote the second letter to her mother almost exactly three years later, she was still reeling from a series of events, most of them tragic, that had struck her and Clemens's lives within months after their wedding. On the most immediate level, Langdon's letter to her mother was responding to the recent death of her grandmother,

135

to a run of bad weather, cranky children, and a houseguest who so "monopolizes Mr. Clemens . . . that I have scarcely seen him today." Her petulance in response to local events was unusual; generally she was more sanguine. But Langdon had valid cause for depression beyond her short-term trials. By this night, two weeks short of her second anniversary, she and Clemens had already weathered more genuine crises than many couples confront in the entire course of their marriages.

Between February 2, 1870, the day they were married, and May 17, 1873, when they sailed on their first trip to Europe together, Langdon and Clemens had two children, moved three times, buried three relatives and one close friend, and endured frequent separations. When Clemens decided that he did not like editing the Buffalo *Express* he quit, thus abandoning one of his few steady jobs. Meanwhile, Langdon had been seriously ill with typhoid fever. As they grappled with these trials, they also dealt with bouts of irritating if nonthreatening illnesses, unsatisfactory servants, and a fractious and worrisome first child. Far from the haven of tranquillity Clemens had imaged in his courtship letters, the first years of their marriage were a crucible in which literary evenings by the fire were an increasing rarity. The story of Langdon and Clemens's first three years of married life is less about a honeymoon than about their struggle to gain control over themselves and outward circumstances.

Langdon and Clemens were married in her parents' parlor on February 2, 1870 and, accompanied by most of the wedding party, they immediately left for their new home in Buffalo. Clemens had been living there since early the previous fall, after buying, with Jervis Langdon's help, a one-third interest in the Buffalo *Express*. Unknown to Clemens, who had fretted about where he and his bride would live and had asked an associate to find them an appropriate boarding house, the Langdons had bought and furnished a house for them in a fashionable section of town, complete with three servants, a stable, "a hot supper on the table and a horse and carriage with their monogram on the panel," according to Charles Dudley Warner.[1] Langdon was in on the secret (as was everyone but Clemens), and when the "boarding house" to which he directed their hack turned out to be a well-appointed town house, filled with laughing friends and new relations, he admitted himself the butt of an excellent joke.

Jeffrey Steinbrink has told the story of Clemens's professional development during the Buffalo years in *Getting To Be Mark Twain*. During this time, he demonstrates, Clemens "sorted out" the elements of his professional character that would go into the making of "Mark Twain" and began the process of self-creation that we, seeing him retrospectively, tend to assume had been there all along. Some of his decisions had to do with his experiences at the *Express*, with other publications for which he was writing, and with his lecture tours; others reflect his aspirations for respectability and his responses to his new in-laws. As he did so professionally, he also developed personally, evolving from the footloose bachelor who thought he wanted to stay home to the Victorian husband who discovered that mandatory business trips can relieve domestic anxieties.

And the new couples' anxieties were often terrible. Langdon and Clemens actually lived in Buffalo only fifteen months, decamping to Elmira in March 1871 and then moving to Hartford in October of that year. In the beginning, Buffalo looked extremely promising, especially as a setting for domestic happiness. The young couple's first letters to their family and friends continuously marvel over the beauties of the new house, which they saw as a kind of fairy palace created just for them. Even Clemens, whom we tend not to think of in terms of household arrangements, was given to rhapsodizing over the furniture and the *objets*. "Samuel said yesterday that it was well that there was no one with us now, because they might be almost surprised [*sic*] at our constant exclamations of delight – when he looked in at our bedroom the other morning, he said that he fairly *started* at seeing the beauty of it," Langdon reported to her parents four days after the wedding (February 6, 1870, MTP). Initially the house served the function all good Victorian homes were supposed to serve – it provided a safe space for its owners to begin to know each other. Built on a complex interplay of intellectual, emotional, and material forces, upper-class Victorian American marriages used material goods as signs of aesthetic and at times even spiritual worth. The statue, the picture, the arrangement of rooms, provided men and women with a common project and encouraged them to discuss their preferences. In the process they came to know and appreciate one another, and the harmony of their domestic space, ideally at least, reflected their relationship.

But this couple's domestic idyll was short. By April, Jervis Langdon's health, on the wane for several years, had seriously deteriorated, and Clemens and Langdon went to Elmira to help nurse him. He died of stomach cancer on August 6. Emma Nye, one of Langdon's Elmira friends, returned with her to Buffalo only to immediately succumb to typhoid fever; with hired help, Langdon also nursed her until she died. Exhausted by these duties, Langdon went into labor one month earlier than expected and gave birth to a son on November 7. Not only premature but prenatally exposed to opiates administered to relieve his mother's stress, the baby, named Langdon, was a frail, difficult infant who wailed much of the day and night and whom most observers did not expect to live. Unable to nurse him herself, his mother spent long days in the Buffalo hospital having him wet-nursed by a woman who had recently given birth there. "She is a nice person and well recommended," Langdon told Alice Hooker Day. "So every day, baby, nurse, and I come up here and spend the day[,] returning home at night." Leaving her fairy palace to sojourn in the medical environment provided for the poor, she noted that "it is about the forlornest place that ever you saw" (January 28, 1871, MTP). In February Olivia contracted typhoid and was helpless for several months. The house that was supposed to be a haven of peace and tranquillity was in fact never quiet; family and friends, invited during the good times, stayed to help during the bad; doctors and nurses swarmed through the rooms. By the time he put the house and his share of the *Express* on the market in the spring of 1871, Clemens had come to loathe Buffalo, and Langdon, too, was happy to leave. Yet through these months, their subsequent hiatus in Elmira, and their first years in Hartford, they began to mature together, striking the tones and setting the patterns for the thirty-four years they would be married. This entailed both developing their emotional relationship and acquiring skills that would enable them to play their roles as wealthy, upper-middle-class Americans. In many ways, Langdon's job was newer and more difficult than her husband's. Whereas Clemens, for all his professional flip-flops, continued doing essentially the same things he had been doing for years – writing, editing, and lecturing – Langdon had not only to learn new skills but also to develop a new sense of self. Essentially, she moved from being a possession over which others contended – the jewel that Clemens sought to steal from her parents – to becoming emotionally self-possessed. Her most obvious move, from being her father's daughter to being her husband's wife, was accompanied by her move from being her mother's daughter into becoming in effect, her own mother: a skilled hostess, an active parent, and an organized, involved, and helpful wife. To become "a woman" in this schema entailed learning how to read, interpret, and respond to a multitude of social, financial, material, and emotional codes. During the first three years of her marriage, Langdon did so; by the time she left for Europe in May 1873, leaving plans for the Hartford house in her architect's hands, she had mastered her environment.

Langdon's major challenge during these years was to develop confidence in her ability to control her environment. This meant, finally, the ability to act without external guidance, human or divine. As noted earlier, for all her early piety, Langdon's professions of dependence on God cease to be evident fairly soon after her marriage. Within the framework set by her early letters to Alice Hooker and the 1869 letter to Mary Fairbanks quoted at the beginning of the chapter, her 1872 letter to her mother is notable for its lack of reference to God. For all her sense of weakness and inadequacy, Langdon did not say she was praying for guidance. She looked to her mother for comfort, and then to herself for strength, "try[ing] earnestly," to tap her own resources rather than a supernatural source. The passages about self-reliance quoted in her commonplace book began, perhaps, to have immediate relevance during these years.

Langdon's falling away from God seems to have been integral to her emergence as Clemens's wife. It is doubtful that Clemens's own skepticism directly influenced her – true to his earlier vows, he seems to have attended church fairly regularly, both at home and on lecture tours.[2] Additionally, Langdon's own poor attendance was in part attributable to her frequent illnesses. But Clemens's courting strategy to trick Langdon into "digging" herself a "matrimonial pit" while trying to convert him seems to have paid extra dividends. The threat secular love poses to religious sensibilities is that the beloved object will take God's place, and this seems to have been what happened to Langdon. Her shift, and her sensitivity to it, are evident in a letter she wrote to Clemens from Hartford late in 1871, recording a visit to church that day.

> It is so long since I have been to church that I was mellowed by the very atmosphere I think, Mr. Twichells prayer touched me and made me cry, he prayed particularly for those who had fallen away and were longing to come back to God – Youth I am ashamed to go back, because I have fallen away so many times and gone back feeling that if I ever should grow cold again, it would be useless trying . . . it would seem if I did not remain steadfast after such times, I never could.

Later in the letter she mentions having heard one of the Warners speak of her own "lukewarmness toward God." When her friend[3] notes that she has decided that having emotional consistency toward God is no more necessary than having it toward one's husband, Langdon reports that she "told her if I felt toward God as I did toward my husband I should never be in the least troubled – I did not tell her how almost perfectly cold I am toward God" (*MTL* 4: 516). Clearly the passion that had fueled Langdon's piety before her marriage has moved into other channels.

Her sexual relationship with Clemens was one of them. Langdon became pregnant within two months of marrying, and she was pregnant again by the time they moved to Hartford in the fall of 1871. Her letters to Clemens during his absences are at least as passionate as his courtship letters to her. Coming from a family that was, though well within the parameters of nineteenth-century decorum, nevertheless fairly easy about sexuality, and having been exposed all her life to sexually outspoken women such as Isabella Hooker and Rachel Gleason, Langdon does not seem to have brought many sexual inhibitions to the marriage. Clemens's well-known letter to his friend Will Bowen, written during the early days of their marriage and marveling over the fact that he had his very own wife, at that moment upstairs in a bed "that I sleep in every night," may express his discovery that his angelic fiancée could be an unexpectedly earthy companion (*MTL* 4: 51). Both sexually active and biologically fertile, Langdon's emotional life was quickly and deeply engaged by Clemens and their children, especially the first, fragile baby. The volatility of her new family engaged the passions that her cooler natal family had not tapped, and the energies that she had directed to religious pieties prior to marriage reoriented shortly after. Her conversations with her friend reveal her discovery that her religious and her sexual passions had the same source.

Langdon's "coldness" toward God, however, created a vacuum in her sense of control over her environment. One of the advantages of knowing God immediately and emotionally is that such certainty provides an interpretive framework for understanding the relationships between self and world, providing rationales for apparently arbitrary events. Without this framework the world can be a cold place, and new experiences can be hard to process. For most, substitute frameworks are imperative.

It has long been common to observe that the nineteenth century saw the removal of God from the center of mainstream American consciousness to its margins. Even while the practice of religion remained strong, perhaps especially as public discourse, its experience as a psychological immediacy became less frequent and, even more important, less valued. Other experiences, other frameworks, had to substitute for the interpretive framework that had been God. Like many of her contemporaries for whom human emotional networks took the place of experiential religion, the framework Langdon developed was compounded of a secularized sense of duty and an ethic of care focused on her family and closest childhood friends. Rather than a theological framework, she developed a familial network that, in tandem with her still-extant if cooler relationship to the church, helped her negotiate her relationship to her environment. During this period the interpretive strategies that she had applied to her reading of literary texts also became the strategies enabling her to "read" her world, and she began to build the communities she had studied in history and fiction. Unlike the relationships on which she had focused in her reading, however, the communities she created were overwhelmingly female.

Langdon's need for human, especially female, networks was evident long before her marriage, especially in her letters to Alice Hooker, where she constantly lamented Alice's absence, berated her for not writing frequently enough, and laid plans for reunions. This activity continued during her engagement, even in letters to relatively new friends such as Mary Fairbanks, where she constantly sought promises that the Fairbanks family would visit Elmira. Certainly she was not unusual in this; most nineteenth-century women's letters openly express their longings for companionship. Both conventional courtesies and a genuine desire for immediate community fueled their invitations to one another. Not surprisingly, passionate importunities were directly proportionate to distance of separation, perhaps one of our best indications of the psychological strain imposed by Americans' ever-increasing mobility. The loss of familiar voices was the hardest part of removal.

Like her contemporaries, Langdon wanted to take her friends with her as she moved. She began inviting family and friends to visit her in Buffalo shortly after her wedding, and her letters written between 1870 and 1873 indicate that she was, in fact, rarely without friends from home. Her passionate declarations of loneliness to her absent husband referred specifically to *his* absence; she was almost never home with only the children and servants. Even when he was present the house was full: "We have the Spaulding girls with us from Elmira, and also the Gleasons from the Water Cure," Clemens wrote to James Redpath shortly after he returned from his lecture tour in 1872, and added: "I wish we had you & your tribe" (February 13, 1872, MTP). Like Langdon, he enjoyed a full house, not even objecting to Clara Spaulding's company on their trip to England in 1873.

For Clemens, however, a house full of company signaled little more profound than a continuous party, whereas for Langdon, it familiarized new environments. One of the functions of familiar faces is to provide a buffer between the individual and his or her new situation. Like most women of her time, Langdon was happiest when other women, preferably familiar ones, mediated between her and her public life. Her letters show her creating this community, and what look to us like strange dependencies actually exhibit Langdon's strategy to create a psychological bridge between herself and the unfamiliar. Clearly capable not only of adapting to new circumstances but also of changing and expanding her horizons, she was uncomfortable doing so without a protective shell of friends. Surrounded by them, she could create a home, a safe and familiar space, and then proceed to normalize the alien territories beyond it.

Langdon's letters to her family from Buffalo show her creating this familiar environment. Within the first two weeks of the couple's residence in their new home, Clemens's sister Pamela Moffett and her daughter Annie came to stay while searching for a place to live in the region. Also that month, Langdon began urging her parents to visit. By April, Clemens mentions that Allie and Clara Spaulding had just completed a ten-day visit and had left in part "because we were beginning to look for my tribe from St. Louis. In which case we should want both spare rooms" (*MTL* 4: 110) – that is, a return visit from the Moffets. This kind of hospitality continued until Emma Nye died while visiting them in

September 1870; it resumed again after their son Langdon's birth in November and continued after their move to Hartford in the fall of 1871.

During the first few months of her marriage, Langdon wrote to her parents nearly every day, continuing the epistolary pattern she and Clemens had developed during their engagement. Affirming that she was happy and not lonely, she nevertheless urged visits and noted that part of her contentment stemmed from the fact that Clemens was accompanying her on her obligatory social calls. Moreover, although one letter suggests that she did go out alone to shop (February 9, 1870, MTP), most ask Elmirans to send her things she needs, from "one or two old warm table cloths to wrap bread and the like in" to "a slip of ivy to train for the dining room window" (February 6, 1870, MTM). With a touch of the kind of humor that we associate with her husband rather than with her, she even sent home for the right kind of cat: "Susie dear, will you send us a couple of cats by the next minister or other party that is coming this way. We have not a cat on the place, and the mice will not patronize the little trap because it is cheap & small & uncomfortable & not in keeping with the other furniture of the house. If you could send us a kitten or two like 'Livy,' it would suit Mr. Clemens's idea of what a house cat should be" (*MTL* 4: 108). True to her family's habits, Langdon counted on the railroads to bring her domestic goods she did not trust Buffalo to provide.

Although both the need for home companions and the emphasis on materials goods was a constant in Langdon's letters to her family and close friends, the contexts in which her protestations of loneliness appeared began to change after she and Clemens moved to Hartford, where she clearly felt more comfortable than in Buffalo. Hartford represented a new start for them both. They had made few real friends in Buffalo, though everyone was friendly; in Hartford they already knew at least half a dozen couples, including Clemens's brother and sister-in-law, Orion and Mollie Clemens; Langdon's friend Alice, now married to John Day; and the two Warner brothers, George and Charles Dudley, with their wives, Lilly and Susan. Clemens's ministerial buddy Joe Twichell was part of their circle, as was his wife, Harmony, and Mary Hooker Burton, Alice Hooker's sister. Isabella and John Hooker, whose house Langdon and Clemens rented until their own was built, were reassuring presences, and, though much older, Isabella's sister Harriet, with her husband Calvin Stowe, also formed part of their growing Hartford coterie.

Langdon's letters from Hartford during her first year there do not stop importuning family and friends to visit. Nor do her missives to her absent husband (Clemens left on a lecture trip almost as soon as they reached Connecticut, traveling from October 1871 through January 1872) cease lamenting his absence. Not surprisingly, these letters are often more weary than those she wrote during her first four months in Buffalo. But they also show a much larger horizon of activity and expectation, and most important, they show Langdon developing a more certain sense of the relationship between herself and her world. Though she would have one more early trial before her – her son would die in June of the following year – Langdon's move to Hartford marked the end of the most tumultuous period of her early marriage and the beginning of her emergence into the world as a self-confident adult female.

The transition was not always smooth. The handful of letters surviving from Langdon's correspondence with Clemens during his lecture tour of 1871–2 show her uncomfortable with her role as Nook Farm wife in her husband's absence, and also still trying to juggle – and make sense of – her many conflicting allegiances. Even more than before, she lamented Clemens's absence, in part because her Hartford acquaintances demanded that she spend more time beyond the confines of her own home: "I do hope that this will be the last season that it will be necessary for you to lecture, it is not the way for a husband and wife to live," she told him on November 20, 1871. A few paragraphs later she added, "I am going over to 'the club' [presumably the Monday Evening Club] now in a few minutes. I wish you were going with me I rather dread it. I want you along to protect me" (*MTL* 4: 499).

A few days later she asked him to pray for her, even though she herself was "not as prayerful as of old." (*MTL* 4: 506).

In addition to her trepidation over solo social appearances, Olivia also worried about the relationship between her husband and her son. A fretful, never fully healthy child, who at sixteen months could not walk,[4] baby Langdon may have been more of a disruptive than a bonding force between his parents. Although Clemens's initial letters to friends after the baby's birth glow with pride, he soon ceased referring to "the cub" much beyond commenting that he cried a lot, comments thinly masked by a humor that barely disguised his irritation. "We don't dare to expose the cub to any more influences calculated to keep him up nights," he told Mary Fairbanks in January 1871. "He did well, last night – was peaceable, and I let him off and didn't 'go for' him with Dewees' Mustang liniment" (*MTL* 4: 314). Two months later he was less controlled: "I believe if that baby goes on crying 3 more hours this way I will butt my frantic brains out and try to get some peace," concludes a letter to Elisha Bliss, Jr., that is signed "Yours, in *perfect* distraction" (*MTL* 4: 366). Once started on his 1871–2 lecture tour, his loving regards to "our boy" in letters to his wife often sound perfunctory – as if he were remembering the child only to please her. Langdon's own letters suggest that his indifference worried her: "The baby is so sweet and dear," she told Clemens on November 20, "I know as he grows older you and he will love each other like *every thing*" (*MTL* 4: 499). Clemens was aware of her anxieties about his relationship with his son, but he did not seem interested in doing much about it in the short term: "Bless your heart, *I* appreciate the cubbie," he reassured her on November 15. "& shall, more & more as he develops and becomes vicious & interesting" (*MTL* 4: 491). His protestations were clearly unsatisfactory. "If anything happens to me you must love him *awfully*," Langdon admonished her husband later that month, anticipating her next labor (November 28, 1871, MTP). The following month she tried to flatter Clemens into appreciating his son's intelligence: "When we say where is papa he looks right at your picture" (December 20, 1871, MTP), and shortly afterward she reiterated her anxieties: "If anything happens to me in the Spring you must never let him go away from you. Keep him always with you, read and study and play with him, and I believe we should be reunited in the other world" (*MTL* 4: 523).

Olivia Susan Clemens was born safely on March 19, 1872, a healthy, lively infant from whose birth her mother soon recovered. Less than three months later baby Langdon succumbed to diphtheria, dying on June 2. Legend has long held that Clemens blamed himself for his son's death, for having neglected to keep him covered during a carriage ride. Contemporary accounts do not mention this. Neighbor Lilly Warner has left probably the most objective account of baby Langdon's death. On June 3, 1872 she wrote her absent husband that "the little Clemens boy has at last finished his weary little life. For two or three days his cold grew worse, till at last, Sat'dy, it was pronounced to be diphtheria, & at 6 o'cl yesterday morning he gave up his life-long struggle to live & died quietly in his mother's arms." In contrast to Albert Bigelow Paine's record of Clemens's guilt, Warner's letter indicates that the father, with the rest of the community, recognized that the child's death was for the best.

> Of course everybody thinks what a mercy that he is at rest – but his poor devoted mother is almost heart-broken. It is always so, I believe – those children that are the most delicate & the [*sic*] needs the most care – that everybody else wants to have die – are the most missed & mourned by their mothers. . . . Mr. Clemens was all tenderness but full of rejoicing for the baby – said he kept thinking it was'nt [*sic*] death for him but the beginning of life. *She* will see it all by & by, but can't yet, & it is such a mercy that they have the little baby. She is strong & well, & an uncommonly pretty baby.

Later that night Warner reiterated her opinion that the death was not tragic. The beautiful spring weather, she remarked, made it seem "as if birds & flowers & sunshine – everything – were rejoicing over that dear little fellow's escape from sorrow & pain." Briefly noting that Clemens's brother Orion and Olivia's sister and brother-in-law, Susan and Theodore Crane, were taking the baby to the Langdon burial plot in Elmira, Warner added, "Aunt Belle [Isabella Hooker] has been a great comfort to them – was with them Sat. night & has been nearly ever since, taking charge of things in her energetic & most kind way." In the end Warner's detachment broke down. After describing Joseph Twichell's "simple & most appropriate" funeral prayer given in the Clemenses parlor among a small group of friends,[5] she told her husband that "I staid last of all & put things back in their own places, & then came home to my own precious little well children. Oh, how sweet & lovely the baby seems & how my heart ached for those who must give up theirs."[6]

An unusually large gap in Clemens's letters, from May 26 to June 11, 1872, suggests the turmoil of this period. When he did write again, his references to baby Langdon's death were carefully distanced. "Our eldest child remained precariously sick for more than two months, & finally died a week ago," he told a friend in his first missive after the death (June 11, 1872, MTP). "Thank you . . . for expressing your kindly . . . sympathy for our irreparable loss," he told Louise Moulton a week later, in a letter that suggests he was responding to comments in her own. "When we shall feel 'reconciled,' God only can tell" (June 18, 1872, MTP). Sandwiched between these letters was one other, a comic – almost manic – letter to Howells so detached from Clemens's current reality as to stand almost as a literary work rather than a personal letter. The paucity – first of letters and second of references to his son's death – together with an unusual formality in what little he did say about it and the carnivalesque release implied by his letter to Howells, suggest that Clemens had not come to terms with his own reactions to baby Langdon's death. Clearly never enamored of his backward son, he probably felt guilty about his relief that the boy was dead – a relief, as Lilly Warner notes, shared by everyone except Olivia. His silence suggests his personal confusion.

If Langdon wrote letters during the spring of 1872 they have disappeared. The first we have from her are written from the beach community of Old Saybrook, Connecticut, to which the family had retired for the season (the first of their many escapes from the heat and fevers of the Hartford summer). Writing to her sister-in-law Mollie, who was staying in the Clemens's rented house in Hartford, Langdon sent a series of requests, all so peremptory and petty that it is well to remember that her emotional state was not conducive to fine considerations. "Dear Mollie, Will you send the little strainer. There are two of them one has a handle and one has not, the one *without* the handle is the one that we want" (undated, 1872, MTM, Chester Davis Estate). "I find that I shall need my black silk long skirt . . . we are very much in need of a new baby-bottle – will you please send one right away . . . "(Thursday morning, 1872, MTM, Chester Davis Estate). "I dropped one of my gold studs in the bath room it went under the bureau I could not find it and forgot to have one of the girls look for it" (July 7, 1872, MTP). These letters show Langdon at her most demanding. More interesting, they show her plunging herself into trivia. Here the material world became a barrier against other kinds of consciousness; things took the place of feeling. When she focused on her lost stud or on Susy's puffed dress, she blocked out baby Langdon's absence. Intermittently, however, she slipped, revealing the longing her obsessions disguised: "Seeing the mother's [*sic*] with their children does make me so homesick for Langdon – it seems as if I could not do without him – Mollie don't let that green box in the closet of the study be touched, it has the cast of Langdon's face in it" (July 7, 1872, MTP). Not only was she grieving, she was self-conscious about being an object of pity: "The only disagreeableness is that there are so many Hartford people in here, out there [*sic*] I stay closely in the room" (ibid.). Erecting a wall of the material, Olivia used Victorian culture to shield herself both from her own emotions and the unwelcome sympathies of others.

These were her worst days, an experience of intense grief not to be repeated until her daughter Susy's death in 1896. At the same time, however, Langdon's horizons were expanding. By renting Isabella and John Hooker's house, the Clemenses established themselves in the "Nook Farm" community, a geographically and socially close group of fairly sophisticated people. Better read and better traveled than any other group she had known on a long-term basis (her sojourns in New York and at various sanitariums had certainly brought her into contact with many cosmopolites, but her contacts with them were relatively brief), this group became Langdon's entrée into the international world. Coming to Hartford this time as wife, not daughter, she not only brought old friends with her but also entered a network of new friends who became part of her continuing education.

Much of this educational activity looked familiar. As in Elmira, Hartford intellectuals formed reading groups, presented papers, and traded new novels. Hartford also offered ample opportunity for formal study through private courses. The difference, one suspects, lay in the degree of sophistication of Langdon's closest associates and in their proximity to the sources of culture. Whereas the Elmira literati were well traveled and familiar with much of the latest thought, many among the Hartford group were *producers* of new ideas. Socializing with the members of the Monday Evening Club, for instance, meant coming into contact with Horace Bushnell, Charles Dudley Warner, James H. Trumbull (an extraordinarily erudite classical scholar), and Calvin Stowe, as well as, of course, Mark Twain, Joseph Twichell, and a number of lawyers, manufacturers, and bankers. Like the Elmira Academy of Science, the club debated topics that had been previously assigned, and specific members were appointed to deliver papers (Twain presented "Facts Concerning the Recent Carnival of Crime in Connecticut" on January 24, 1876). Although women did not officially participate in the meetings, according to a recent historian of the club, "the wife of the host was always invited and it was customary for her to ask several friends to sit with her, usually in the hall or on the stairs. Crackers, cheese, and beer gradually became a so-called 'light supper' at ten o'clock."[7] Apparently, this was the meeting to which Langdon was headed on November 20, 1871, when she wished her husband was there to "protect" her; a November 15 letter from Lilly Warner to her husband notes that "Charley [her brother-in-law] has the club there Monday evening – at which the Labor question is to be discussed. Susy said she . . . particularly wanted Mrs. Clemens, she being a stranger there."[8] Sitting on the stairs or in the hall, Langdon would have been in the familiar situation of being grouped with intelligent women (some of whom, like Lilly Warner and Harriet Beecher Stowe, were writers themselves) whose sex marginalized them from formal events but did not prevent them from voicing their opinions in other arenas – most likely, in this situation, at the "light supper" that they (or rather, their servants) gave their husbands at 10:00 P.M. Initially fearful, Langdon eventually became one of the best-known hostesses of this group and a participant in both its serious debates and in its notorious fun. Seeing herself as a facilitator rather than a producer of new ideas, her skills lay in arranging, easing, and conversing, in designing the stage for the actors and, at times, in directing the play. Universally admired, both for her personality and her hospitality, she was one of the nineteenth-century American women who had the money, leisure, and intelligence to develop the role of wife to a high art.

Among the Hartford literati, this would have been impossible had she not been able to compete intellectually. Although many of her contemporaries stopped reading after they married, Langdon was encouraged to continue improving herself. At first, much of this was done in tandem with visits from relatives and close friends. "Mother and I have finished *The United Netherlands* and commenced Dickens' *Childs History of England,*" she wrote Clemens on November 28, 1871.

It is written in the very simplest style, we read this evening only one chapter of 6 or 7 pages and it went over all the time of the rule of the Romans, the Druids, and so on, I am afraid if that chapter is a fair sample that it is almost too condensed, I am fond of that time of the Druidical religion, and wanted to hear more of it – There is more in the Cyclopedia than is given there – But I presume after the Norman Conquest that it will not be quite so condensed. (*MTL* 4: 505, n8)

Langdon Clemens, b. 11/7/1870; d. 6/2/1872. Mark Twain Archives, Elmira College.

(*opposite, top*) John and Isabella Beecher Hooker House, Hartford, exterior with croquet players. Tentative identifications, left to right: seated, unidentified; John Hooker; unidentified woman; unidentified woman; George or Charles Warner; Lilly Warner; seated, Mary or Alice Hooker. Harriet Beecher Stowe Center, Hartford, Connecticut.

(*opposite, bottom*) Mark Twain House, exterior, 1874–81. The Mark Twain House, Hartford, Connecticut.

153

Mark Twain House, interior, library, *c.* 1874. The house is new and not yet fully furnished. The Mark Twain House, Hartford, Connecticut.

Mark Twain House, interior, library looking onto the conservatory, *c.*
1896. The Mark Twain House, Hartford, Connecticut.

Quarry Farm, 1874. From left to right: unidentified servant, probably a German nurse, seated, holding Susy Clemens; Samuel L. Clemens; Susan Crane; Theodore Crane; unidentified standing servant; Olivia Langdon Clemens, holding Clara Clemens; unidentified standing servant; Rachel Cord (seated, elevated); unidentified seated servant. In the rear is Olivia Lewis Langdon's coachman and his wagon. The octagonal study is on the hill in the background. The Mark Twain House, Hartford, Connecticut.

(*opposite, top*) Family Photo. From left to right: Susan (Susie) Clemens, Cat (surname unknown), Jean Clemens, Olivia Langdon Clemens, Clara Clemens. Mark Twain Archives, Elmira College.

(*opposite, bottom*) Clemens in his octagonal study at Quarry Farm, probably mid-1870s. Mark Twain Archives, Elmira College.

157

The context of this literary critique is one of the letters in which Langdon worried about performing her domestic role and voiced her hopes for their family's future. Similarly, a December 31, 1871 letter fervently expressing her love for Clemens also noted that "Clara Sue and Theodore are here, Sue and Theodore are just now looking over Raynard the fox, Clara is looking at Fallstaff [*sic*] and his friends, (Paul Konewewka's Silhouetts [*sic*] that I gave Mother for Christmas)" (*MTL* 4: 523, n2). In the same letter she noted, "I am going down this morning to see about a German teacher, we are going to begin German right away." Sounding like Alice Hooker four years earlier, she commented that "Clara and I mean to read and study and do *every thing.*" In Buffalo, shortly after baby Langdon's birth, she had written Alice Hooker Day that "Mr Clemens and I read with a great deal of pleasure Mr Warner's book – I came very near writing Mrs Warner and telling her of the two or three exceedingly pleasant evenings that the book gave us" (January 25, 1871, MTP) and shortly after her second child was born in Elmira, her husband wrote Charles and Susan Warner that "we have read two Back-logs [essays slated to be published in Warner's 1873 collection *Back-Log Studies*] aloud since we came here, & a thoroughly grateful audience have insisted both times that I write & cordially thank the author." He went on to suggest that Langdon was concerned because she had not yet returned to her own studies.[9] Rather than ignoring education for more domestic concerns, Langdon found her literary interests encouraged by her new environment, and her critiques became increasingly sophisticated.

As in their courtship letters, Clemens also encouraged Langdon's literary pursuits through his reports of his own reading on his lecture tours. Although he protested that "I don't get a *chance* to read anything, my old darling – am patching at my lecture all the time," he not only did read but marked passages for her and critiqued his reading. "I'm *going* to mark Lowell for you," he promised on November 15, 1871 (*MTL* 4: 491). Shortly before, he had found time to read "*Eugene Aram* [on the train] all day -- found it tedious – skipped 4 pages out of 5. Skipped the corporal *all* the time. He don't amount to *anything*" (*MTL* 4: 483). "I am reading 'The Member from Paris,' a very bright, sharp, able French political novel, very happily translated," he told her at the beginning of 1872. "It is all so good and so Frenchy that I don't know where to mark! I have read and sent home *The Golden Legend, The New England Tragedies, Edwin of Deira, Erling the Bold*, and a novel by the author of *John Halifax* – forgotten the name of it."[10] Langdon received and responded to at least one of these gifts: "I think the Golden Legend is beautiful I wonder you did not mark it still more than you have," she told him; "I do so heartily enjoy the books that you have marked" (January 7, 1872, MTP). A week later Clemens sent a letter that suggests one way the dynamics of the Nook Farm intellectual circle worked. "I enclose a poem – or rather, two poems," he noted on January 20.

> The woman's poem is exquisite – Mr. Longfellow's is not to be mentioned in the same day with it. But Mr. L has not plagiarized. If he had been stealing from this woman he would not have overlooked one of her finest points – the one where the old Monk's simple sense of *duty* makes him spring up & go to his charitable work when the bells ring – Longfellow makes him drag himself reluctantly away in answer to a plain call 'within his breast' – a call so worded as to give the instant impression that he recognized in it a command, (& a *promise*, almost,) from the Vision. I have seen this beautiful old legend put into all manner of poetical measure, but never so touchingly & effectively as this woman has done it. Show it to Warner. (January 20, 1872, MTP)

We can imagine this letter and the poems accompanying it moving from Clemens to Langdon to Charles Dudley Warner and, probably, from Warner at least to Susan Warner, his wife, and Lilly Warner, his literary sister-in-law. It could well have also been shown to Joe and Harmony Twichell, the Clemens's ministerial friends. Materials and a critique, resulting in dissemination of the materials and, doubtlessly, a debate involving aesthetics, poetics, history, and theology – these, even more than the formalities of the Monday Evening or Saturday Morning clubs, were the core of the Nook Farm intellectual circle.

Additionally, a major educational factor for both Langdon and Clemens was the continuing process of book production in their own home. Mark Twain critics have made much negative noise about Langdon having excised any language or scenes that would not qualify as parlor literature, but as Jeffrey Steinbrink and Guy Cardwell have observed, they did not take into consideration Clemens's own desire to transform himself into a professional writer during this period. That meant, in part, learning to detect and delete passages whose crudity would not pass muster with reviewers from major magazines, especially family-oriented ones. In an era in which the family became a cultural icon, and a multitude of popular outlets – written, visual, and dramatic – appeared to uphold and exploit the national obsession, writers aiming for a wide popular audience were forced to observe popular standards. The rewards were rich: "The 'Innocents Abroad' (now 3 1/2 years old) sold 12,000 copies this last year – sells . . . 1000 a month right along – which looks as if it had entered permanently into the literature of the country," Clemens told Whitelaw Reid with satisfaction (April 20, 1873, MTP).

Hence Langdon – in the interstices between housekeeping, entertaining, childbearing, letter writing, and other wifely duties – did listen to and make comments on the three books Clemens produced between their engagement and their first trip to England. Like her contact with the other Hartford literati, this demanded a daily expenditure of real intellectual energy – no longer simply absorbing, or being the most intellectual respondent in her Elmira circle, here she was asked for continual creative input. Her ability to do so was one of the factors fueling her maturation. The woman who left for England on the *Batavia* knew she was part of a productive relationship that had impact on the world.

For Clemens, of course, the process of constant writing paid off in much more visible terms. Steinbrink has argued persuasively that the Buffalo years saw Sam Clemens transformed into

Mark Twain – a conscious, deliberate, and difficult movement from newspaper humorist into serious writer. Clemens's evident satisfaction with *The Innocents Abroad*'s impact – and sales – suggests that he liked seeing himself in this role. His next long work, *Roughing It*, was written during the most difficult months of the Buffalo experience and finished, gratefully, during the 1871 hiatus in Elmira. *The Gilded Age*, Twain's first long fiction, written in collaboration with neighbor Charles Dudley Warner, had difficulties of other kinds, most stemming from the tricky process of collaboration itself. But it, too, ended with satisfaction for Clemens. Writing almost up to the time the boat left for England, he could tell Whitelaw Reid, who had just run a notice (that Twain disliked) about it in the *Tribune*, that "our novel will have some *point* to it & will *mean* something, & *I* think it will not be snubbed & thrown aside, but will make some men talk, & may even make some people *think*" (April 20, 1873, MTP). From humorist to best-selling author to social critic; these were the developmental stages Mark Twain went through in his professional self-image during the early years of his marriage. The process was emotionally gratifying, and the material rewards were gratifying as well: "Have just bought the loveliest building lot in Hartford 544 feet front on the Avenue & 300 feet deep (paid for it with first six months of 'Roughing It' how's that?)" he first trumpeted, then crossed out, in a letter to Reid at the start of 1873 (January 13 and 17, 1873, MTP).

Learning to see themselves as cultural producers as well as consumers, then, was part of both Samuel and Olivia Langdon Clemens's education. In tandem with all these activities, Langdon also received – or taught herself – an education in the business end of cultural production. Both in Buffalo and in Hartford, Langdon was learning how to be her husband's executive secretary and to oversee – at least theoretically – the family's accounts. It is in her business correspondence both with and for Mark Twain that we see the legacy from her parents, both of whom spent their early years tending shop and keeping accounts. Like many business wives, Langdon realized early in her marriage that she could help herself and her family's life by learning to help Clemens keep his schedules straight and reminding him of his appointments and other obligations. Though Clemens claimed to "hate to have to inflict on you the bore of answering my business letters" (*MTL* 4: 499), Langdon also took over much of his ordinary business correspondence, including the weary demand for autographs. "I answered all your letters today except the one . . . I could not find," she told Clemens on November 20, 1871, the day she was to attend the Monday Evening Club. One of the letters she wrote that day was to an acquaintance, Robert Howland, in response to his request for the date of Twain's reading in Auburn (presumably, Auburn, N.Y.). Noting that the Howlands had visited them in Buffalo, Langdon invited them to "finish your Buffalo visit" in Hartford (November 20, 1871, MTP). The hybrid form of this letter is significant; it shows how instrumental Langdon was in expanding the Clemens's social circle while she conducted business – and vice versa. Though she often chided her husband for his spontaneous invitations to casual acquaintances, she was in fact equally responsible for their ever-expanding circle of guests. In her letter to Howland, punctiliousness about answering Clemens's mail encouraged her hospitality. Autographs were another matter. "I send you a letter of C. B. Plummer," she wrote Clemens the next week. "If you could tell me what to write him I would write for you – I will send him one of your photographs" (November 28, 1871, MTP). The demand for autographs was so persistent that Langdon later had Clemens presign a batch of cards that she could send out on request. She became so efficient as his secretary that by January Clemens was treating her like one: "Sent Ned House's letter back to you for preservation. *Give it to Orion & let him hand it to Bliss to be read – then let Bliss send it back to you. Don't forget*," he ordered from Harrisburg, Pennsylvania (January 21, 1872, MTP).

Becoming her husband's secretary was not a radical activity. As Langdon's parents' early marriage demonstrated, such "working wives" were a common phenomenon among American couples striving to expand business and still keep expenses down. For women, however, participation in husbands' business affairs had the added advantage of pulling them into the public sphere, exposing them to business practices, and giving them a sense of competence in a marketable skill. For Langdon, it was one more sign of her own maturity. Finances, on the other hand, presented a far more difficult problem. In *Nook Farm: Mark Twain's Hartford Circle*, Kenneth R. Andrews notes that "at one time or another, every one of [Nook Farm's] residents had acute financial trouble,"[11] and the saga of the Clemens family's financial reverses is a long and complex one. Neither Clemens nor Langdon had the talent or temperament for long-range management of the large amounts of money that came to them, and it took a bankruptcy and the personal protection of a capitalist baron in the 1890s to finally order their finances. From the beginning, however, Langdon attempted to keep an orderly financial profile, both of her own and her husband's money. Not only was Clemens bringing in a sizable income, she too brought money to the marriage, in the form of material goods such as the Buffalo house and its furnishings, in her shares of Langdon & Co., and in outright gifts from her parents – unsolicited checks for $1,000 were not-infrequent events in the Clemens household.

At the same time, however, household expenses were high, even during the Buffalo period. In a pattern that seems to have repeated itself throughout her life, Langdon would carefully make budgets and then spend large amounts of money on items that had never entered her calculations. A child of parents who had worked their way up from the rural lower middle class, she was at once sensible of the need for monetary restrictions and unable to live within them. Born after her parents' success, she could not envision a time when miraculous checks would not come wafting down from the southern tier.

Langdon was making budgets before she married Clemens. In 1869 she laid out a budget and told him that she was cheap to feed and clothe: "Livy thinks we can live on a very moderate sum & that we'll not need to lecture," Clemens told his mother in June. "I can't scare her by reminding her that her father's family expenses are forty thousand dollars a year, because she produces the documents at once to show that precious little of this outlay is on *her* account" (*MTL* 3: 260). December saw her projecting budgets, almost as a form of doodling: $25 a week for household expenses, $10, $12, and $30 a month for three different kinds of servants, $300 a year for keeping a horse (*MTL* 3: 429, n6). Meanwhile she had counseled Clemens that his intention to help his brother Orion was a blessed one and that they would manage despite the problems it would cause them: "I know that while you are in debt you do not know very well how to spare money, but it is the gifts that really cost us something that are most valuable in Gods sight – We will be the more economical in our way of living, I will look out that I get few dresses and gloves and the like, and we shall be able to help them on." (*MTL* 3: 393, n1). After they were married, Clemens burlesqued her accounts publicly but listened to her privately. "Livy overhauled her books yesterday & demonstrated that our living expenses average exactly fifty dollars a week," he told his in-laws on April 16, 1870. "Other expenses will not amount to more than fifty more, & so we are safe, beyond all peradventure. Every cent of the returns from the book can go to the liquidation of the Express debt if necessary" (*MTL* 4: 110). Already burdened with debt for his share of the Buffalo *Express*, Clemens began his marriage in a state of financial anxiety that made him eager to hear encouraging words from his wife.

In the spring of 1870 Langdon herself was struggling to understand the financial side of household management. Her 1869 projection of $25 per week in household expenses had already doubled, and she was eager to garner whatever monies she could: "Tell Sue that if she wants [a drab poplin dress that Langdon had left in Elmira] I wish she would use it. I don't know whether we could settle as to the price, she may think that $150.00 is a high price but I think if she should look into the merits of that dress she would not think it too much," she wrote her mother (February 20, 1870). In May her parents sent her a check for $1,000; Clemens and Langdon's joint thank-you note indicates that he wanted to use the money for further renovations on the house, whereas she thought they should use it to reduce their debt (May 13, 1870, MTP). A year later they were little better off. Responding to a letter from his relatives in Fredonia, Clemens somewhat defensively noted that "all I made out of the Innocents Abroad was $25,000 & I sunk it in the Buffalo Express – & meantime I have made $25,000 lecturing & in other miscellaneous work – & that I have spent – at least a good deal of it. So far, I have only received $10,500 out of the new book [*Roughing It*]. I have about $20,000 in bank, & Livy about the same. So you see we are not nearly so rich as the papers think we are" (May 17, 1872, MTP). "A Mysterious Visit," a humorous first-person narrative about a visit from a tax assessor, echoes this letter's concerns. Published in March 1870, this sketch features Twain's paradigmatically ignorant and overconfident narrator, who is fooled by a stranger into revealing his true income from sources such as marketing "The Innocents Abroad." In the course of the sketch the narrator is hit with a hefty tax.[12] The U.S. income tax, a Civil War measure not yet repealed, was high, and the autobiographical nature of the sketch suggests how much Clemens's financial anxieties permeated his public and his private lives.

Between 1871 and 1874, the period during which the Clemenses lived in John and Isabella Hooker's house in Hartford while they planned their own house and had it built, both realized that their expenses far outstripped their income, and that much as they disliked them, Clemens's lecture tours were their only way to stay afloat. Even before their own house was built, the bills kept arriving. "The Pottier and Stymus bill has come,"[13] Langdon wrote Clemens on November 20, 1871, immediately after claiming that these separations are "not the way for a husband and wife to live if they can possibly avoid it." She continued: "It is $128.00. I thought it would probably be $150.00 at least. Then the bill on the insurance of our goods against accident – $60.00 – so it is well that you left me the additional $150.00 if you had not I should have run ashore" (*MTL* 4: 499). Two weeks later Langdon was beginning to plan for their new house. Referring to income from her own investments, she declared that she had decided that

> we will put if it is necessary the $29000 into house, grounds, and what new furniture we may need. If we wait to know whether we can afford it we shall wait eight years, because I do not believe we shall know whether we can afford to live in this way until the end of the copartnership – Charlie says I can perfectly well have from there five hundred dollars a month[14] – You may lecture *one month* in New England during the Winter, that will give you $2000.00 that will give you what money you want for Ma and other incidental matters – The three hundred dollars a month with what your regular work will bring you will be plenty.

She ended the subject with a typically optimistic, and increasingly unrealistic, confidence: "If after a time we find that the estate is not worth a living to us, we will change entirely our mode of living." Fortunately, this possibility lay in the distant future:

> That probably will not be discovered for three or four or perhaps the eight years – We shall involve nobody and discomfort nobody, we will not be in debt for our house – The children will then be older and I shall not need so much help in the care of them. I shall then be stronger if I keep on increasing in strength as I have done. We will either board or live in a small cottage and keep one servant, will live near the horse cars so that I can get along without a horse and carriage.

She then brought the subject back to her original objective: "I *can not* and *will not* think about your being away from me this way every year, it is not half living – if in order to sustain our present mode of living you are obliged to do that, then we will change our mode of living" (*MTL* 4: 510–11).

Despite all these plans, the Clemenses continued to outspend their income, and Twain continually went on the lecture circuit – not only in New England between November 1871 and January 1872 (after which he told James Redpath, "I haven't a cent to show for all this long campaign. Squandered it thoughtlessly pay-

ing debts" [January 27, 1872, MTP]), but also in old England
the following year, when the panic of 1873 temporarily wiped out
much of Langdon's income and left them holding only the few
hundred dollars that Langdon's mother and Pamela Moffett had
sent to pay for gifts.[15] By then, Langdon had changed her tune
about the value of lecturing: "Mr. Clemens can lecture and get
money to pay our debts and get us home – now Mother don't
you and Charlie laugh at that, lecturing is what Mr. C. always
speaks of doing when their [*sic*] seems any need of money"
(Thursday, September [n.d.], 1873, MTM). Despite their sudden
poverty, they did not cancel a planned trip to Paris; in the end,
Langdon wrote, they did not think it would make much difference to their economic state. This inability to forego immediate
pleasures for long-term stability was at the heart of both Samuel
and Olivia Clemens's fiscal irresponsibility.

Throughout this period, the two were learning how to be married, to become the couple that would be famous for their house
and hospitality on Farmington Avenue. This entailed not only
learning to control their environment and weathering crises but
also becoming familiar with and sympathetic to each others' interests – exploring each others' worlds. Although critics have generally felt that it was a good thing for Langdon to learn something
about Twain's world (provided she didn't tamper with it), they
have tended to sneer at his forays into hers, denigrating his burgeoning interest in houses, furniture, and Victorian *objets* as undermining his masculinity and pandering to her family's values.
This equation of masculinity with crudity and bourgeois effemi-
nacy with Victorian interiors is far more a function of early twentieth-century critics' conflicts with the generation that preceded
them than of either Clemens's own tastes and values or those of
his contemporaries. Although he occasionally refused to conform
to minor middle-class customs – in one courtship letter he refused
Langdon's request that he wear boutonnieres – generally he was
more than happy to familiarize himself with his era's material
culture. The image of Mark Twain fussing about his clothes and
choosing knicknacks for the parlor has not been much promul-

gated, but that "Twain" also existed, and he was part and parcel of Clemens's intimate life.

Clemens was sending Langdon his laundry and instructions for mailing it back well before the wedding. In the context of the times – that is, a century before washing and drying clothes became a matter of hours rather than days – this was not surprising, since his lecture schedule prevented Clemens from staying anywhere long enough to have his things washed, dried, and ironed. But the Samuel Clemens who masked as an ambling, disheveled Mark Twain turned out to be fairly particular about his clothes, as Langdon discovered not long into her marriage: "Ellen [a servant brought from Elmira] too needs her polishing and fluting irons," Langdon wrote her mother on February 20, 1870, in a letter asking for a number of items to be sent from home, and added: "this Youth of mine does not want his shirts ironed 'till the polishing irons come" (MTM). Two weeks later they had still not arrived, and Clemens, apparently, was getting fidgety. "Mr. Clemens is very anxious to have the polishing irons come I should get some here but they do not seem to keep them. I could not get any. I do not know whether there is any way to hurry them, but the Youth does not like to wear his shirts done up without them" (March 2, 1870, MTM). Two years later Clemens still found time to remember sartorial matters: "Livy darling, did these clothes ever come?" he wrote from Wooster, Ohio.

> If so you ought to have informed me. If they did, forward the enclosed note to the tailors, along with the bill (have Orion get you a check for $89 & enclose that, too – I am out of money). If they *didn't* come, write & tell *Redpath* so . . . & enclose my letter & the draft to *him* & let him see the tailors. (January 7, 1872, MTP)

Mark Twain's clothes, like his lectures and his publications, were clearly a matter to be arranged on a national – or at least a regional – scale.

In addition to his concern for his personal appearance, Clemens entered willingly into the game of furnishing a Victorian

168

house and sporting the emblems of the well-to-do. "Livy darling, my diamonds are a daily & nightly & unceasing delight to me, they are so beautiful," he effused late in 1871. He added: "My shirts are doubtless lying in the Express office, since you don't speak of their arrival" (*MTL* 4: 507). Unquestionably impressed by the magnificence of the Buffalo house given them as a wedding gift by Langdon's parents, Clemens was also quickly taken by the pleasures of ornamenting it, praising the mirrors, pictures, and statues that came as wedding gifts, lamenting the breaking of the statue "Peace" and apparently genuinely happy to see its replacement, and wanting, according to Langdon, to put part of his income into further renovations instead of into his debt for his share in the Buffalo *Express*. Later he would be equally involved in furnishing and decorating the Hartford house. In the interim, he appreciated gifts that beautified the house that he and Langdon rented from the Hookers: "Mother dear, the autumn leaves are *exquisite*, & so is the frame that encloses them," he thanked his mother-in-law late in 1872. "The gift occupies the middle of my study mantel . . . [and gives] the study a dainty air that marvelously assists composition" (December 3, 1872, MTP). Even discounting the mandatory courtesies evident here, it is clear that the author regards his culture's material artifacts with pleasure. Like his contemporaries, his definition of "home" and "comfort" was, in the end, rooted as much physically as spiritually.

Clemens's appreciation of material culture was also part of his developing marriage, that is, one way that he shared his wife's concerns. Throughout their correspondence in these early years, one senses both Clemens and Langdon juggling their own imperatives, struggling, as all new couples do, to discover how much each can exercise his or her own prerogatives and still continue to please the other. Certainly the desire to please accounts for some of Clemens's effusions about material objects, as it does for some of Langdon's protestations of love and longing – a reversal, we must remember, from her carefully refrained courtship letters. At the same time, both parties made clear the boundaries of their own prerogatives: for Clemens, the need, both financial and temperamental, to periodically leave home on lecture tours; for Langdon, the need to maintain familial networks and to create appropriate physical environments. Since these prerogatives were basically antithetical, it was essential for Clemens' and Langdon's marriage that they create areas of common concern. Although the intense materiality of Victorian culture – especially among the wealthy – was far less gendered than twentieth-century critics have assumed, in *this* relationship, Langdon and her family initiated material acquisition, and Clemens (whose peripatetic life had not encouraged accumulation) willingly entered into the sport. Like Langdon's learning to critique his writings, Clemens's learning, with her, to beautify their home provided them with common ground.

The Clemenses' Hartford house, still very much in its planning stages when they left for England in 1873, expressed their joint interests in the material manifestation of their marriage. Additionally for Langdon, designing and furnishing it was another sign of full adulthood. Both parties were enthusiastic about the project, from purchasing the lot to engaging the architect. "I have just bought a lovely piece of ground, 544 feet front on the Avenue here, and 320 deep & shall have a house built in the midst of it while we are absent in England – & then we'll have a blow-out there every time you can run down from Boston," Clemens told John Mouland (January 22, 1873, MTP).[16] Their acquaintances, many of whom were buying similar lots, were equally interested in the Clemenses' purchase. "They would be charming neighbors for us, at least *she* would," Lilly Warner wrote her husband in 1871, when the Clemenses were just beginning to think about buying. "I like her *very* much – a warm-hearted, thoroughly genuine little woman – bright and enthusiastic."[17] Two years later Langdon was showing Warner her plans " 'because Mr. Clemens knew nothing about houses on paper and she *must* talk with somebody about it as they went along' . . . she said she had decided to turn it around . . . she wants to get it all drawn out before they see [an architect]."[18] Always forthright with her opinions, Warner noted that she did not like Langdon's design. Her detailed account of their conversation tells us that Langdon, like her mother nine years earlier, was designing her own house, making sure she had the basic plan completed before turning it over to the experts. Edward T. Potter, the New York architect the Clemenses finally hired, listened to their ideas before completing the nineteen-room, five-bath mansion on which they finally settled. Throughout the house, the tastes, quirks, and priorities of both individuals were manifested in architecture and in ornament.

As the house provided Olivia and her husband with a common interest, so parenting became an arena in which they both participated. While baby Langdon was probably a more divisive than cementing force (certainly one reason Clemens's initial letters from his lecture tour of 1871–2 exhibit such a giddy joy at release from domesticity), the subsequent Clemens children, at least in their early years, provided great pleasure to both parents. With his daughters, one senses, Clemens learned to father. "Wish you all a merry Christmas & many happy returns," he wrote his mother cheerfully, and added: "I have been aggravating the baby by showing her another baby in a hand-glass whom she can't find behind it" (December 20, 1872, MTP). Finally having a child whom he could tease without causing serious physical repercussions, Clemens began to learn how much he could enjoy his children. Never responsible for their formal educations – Langdon did almost all of the researching, hiring, evaluating, and firing of teachers, as well as some of the teaching itself – he nevertheless actively participated in his daughters' intellectual growth and their physical fun. This was especially marked during the years between infancy and adolescence, the relatively genderless years of nineteenth-century childhood, when girls were permitted to romp almost as much as boys. While Langdon taught her daughters basic biology and composition, and engaged tutors for history, modern languages, and other academic subjects, Clemens teased them, invented yard-sized games for them, read to and with them, helped them write and stage plays, and, during their summers at Quarry Farm in Elmira, helped them learn to ride Kadichen, their pet donkey. With Langdon and their servants, he also disciplined them and comforted them during illnesses. His and Langdon's letters and their daughters' reminiscences suggest that the parental jockeying about child rearing was the major positive aspect of the Clemens's marriage in the years between Susy's birth in 1872 (Clara was born in 1874 and Jean in 1880) and her death from spinal meningitis in 1896.

Between February 2, 1870, the day of their wedding, and May 17, 1873, the day they sailed for England on the S.S. *Batavia*, Olivia Langdon and Samuel Clemens began learning how to be married. Staking out territories, establishing patterns of communication and modes of activities and passivities, they exhibited both cultural influences and personal tastes. When Langdon insisted on surrounding herself with a constant stream of family and friends, she knew that women in her culture were expected to live almost entirely social lives; when Clemens expressed relief that his lecture tours forced him to leave the chaotic domesticity such sociability entailed, he knew that men in his culture were expected to make frequent business trips. At the same time, Clemens enjoyed and often encouraged the family's frenetic conviviality, and Langdon frequently retreated to bed to recover from exhaustion. Both found long summers in Elmira imperative for their mental and physical health. Similarly, Langdon learned how to be Mark Twain's secretary as well as Samuel Clemens's wife, while Clemens learned about the material culture so important to Langdon and the rest of their peers. Both learned how to juggle in-laws and to survive the traumas and tragedies of child rearing. Defining their marriage in traditional terms, they negotiated their conjugal as well as their individual relationships to the outside world. The Mr. and Mrs. Clemens who sailed on the S.S. *Batavia* had a fairly good sense of each others' strengths and weaknesses and were beginning to know how and when to exercise control. England would expand their joint horizons, their tastes, and their acquaintances. The relationship that seemed so unlikely in 1868 would last until Langdon's death in 1904.

Throughout the marriage, she and her husband would prove able to create sustaining communities, establish themselves as persons of social and intellectual consequence, and withstand the trials that love, loss, and economic vicissitudes brought them.

NOTES

INTRODUCTION

1. The Langdons were married on July 23, 1832. See "The End of a Noble
   Life," an obituary for Olivia Lewis Langdon, *Elmira Daily Advertiser*, November 29, 1890: 5.
2. Apparently the date of Susan's adoption is unknown. See Gretchen Sharlow, " 'Love to All the Jolly Household': A Study of the Cranes of Quarry
   Farm, Their Lives and Their Relationship with Mark Twain," master's
   thesis, Elmira College, 1991.
3. *Elmira Star Gazette*, June 27, 1939. Langdon biography subfile of the
   Langdon Family file, the Chemung County Historical Society, Elmira,
   New York.
4. Elmira census, August 3, 1860, Chemung County Historical Society.
5. Legal records show that Jervis Langdon bought the Ely property from
   Martha Ely on November 1, 1862. See Chemung Deeds, 44, p. 3. The
   deed does not, however, mention a house. According to the Langdon
   biography subfile of the Langdon family file at the Chemung County
   Historical Society, the Langdon family moved into the house on that
   property in 1865.
6. Olivia Lewis Langdon's Diary, 1865–6, Mark Twain Memorial, Trinity
   College, Hartford, Conn. The diary is dated but not paginated. Subsequent references will be documented internally. Olivia Lewis Langdon's
   diary speaks primarily of interior renovations to this house. While I was
   hunting for photographs for this book, however, I found pictures suggesting that extensive renovations were also made to the exterior. These
   pictures need more investigation than deadlines for this book permit,
   but if they are correctly labeled they suggest that the Ely house, though
   large, was a plain, square, two-and-a-half-story clapboard, and that the

Langdons transformed it into a richly embellished, three-and-a-half-story brownstone.

7. The Chemung Canal, which linked Elmira with Seneca Lake, was completed in 1833 and served the area, with decreasing effectiveness, until it was closed in 1878. During its heyday, the town of Millport (earlier named Millvale) was a major center of boat building. See Catherine S. Connelly, "The Chemung Canal: 19th Century Freightway," *Chemung County Historical Journal*, 1, no. 4 (June 1956): 143–60. Jervis and Olivia Langdon lived in Millport between 1838 and 1845, when they moved to Elmira. See Ausburn Towner, *A Brief History of Chemung County, New York* (New York: Barnes, 1907), 29, n36. One branch of the Underground Railroad ran from Elmira to Watkins Glen, at the head of Seneca Lake; Millport was a logical stopping place along it.

8. In 1870, in a letter to Olivia Lewis three months after Jervis's death, Frederick Douglass wrote, "If I had never seen nor heard of Mr. Langdon since the days that you and himself made me welcome under your roof in Millport, I should never have forgotten either of you. Those were times of ineffaceable memories with me." *Mark Twain's Letters, Volume 3, 1869*, Victor Fischer, Michael B. Frank, and Dahlia Armon, eds. (Berkeley and Los Angeles: University of California Press, 1992), 428, n2. Subsequent references to this volume will be documented internally. The editors of the *Letters* speculate that the Langdons sheltered Douglass on his flight from Maryland, but the editors of the Library of America, which is editing both Twain's and Douglass's collected works, contend that Douglass was already lecturing for the abolitionists and that the Langdons put him up during one of his tours (discussion with Hannah Bercovitch, May 30, 1992). On July 17, 1873, Douglass came to Elmira to speak at a Civil Rights Bill celebration and was again lodged at the Langdon home, this time, of course, guest only of Olivia Lewis. *Chemung County Historical Journal*, 23, no. 4 (June 1978): 2809. On August 9, 1880, Douglass wrote to the Langdons' son Charles in response to a note Charles had sent him. He thanked Charles for his concern for Douglass's welfare – apparently in reference to a lecture tour – and once more recalled the Millport episode and Olivia Lewis as "one . . . who was kind and friendly to me when friends were few and foes were many." Frederick Douglass, letter to Charles Langdon, August 9, 1880, Mark Twain Memorial, Hartford, Connecticut. (Subsequent references to the memorial will be abbreviated MTM.)

9. The story of John W. Jones and the Underground Railroad is part of Elmira lore. With the financial backing of men such as Langdon, Jones "received" up to thirty fugitives a night from employees of the Northern Central Railroad, on its late-night run from Philadelphia. They left at 4

A.M. on the train that went without changing straight through to Niagara. "Underground Railroad: Route to Freedom," *Chemung County Historical Journal*, 6, no. 4 (June 1961): 861–5; and Abner C. Wright, "Underground Railroad Activities in Elmira," *Chemung County Historical Journal*, 14, no. 1 (September 1968): 1755–7.

10. Thomas K. Beecher, eulogy for Olivia Lewis Langdon, Park Church, January 11, 1891.

11. The 1862–3 Elmira College catalog lists Jervis Langdon as one of the trustees.

12. Laura Skandera-Trombley, *Mark Twain in the Company of Women* (Philadelphia: University of Pennsylvania Press, 1994), 73–94.

13. Jeffrey Steinbrink, *Getting To Be Mark Twain* (Berkeley and Los Angeles: University of California Press, 1991).

14. Resa Willis, *Mark and Livy: The Love Story of Mark Twain and the Woman Who Almost Tamed Him* (New York: Atheneum, 1992).

15. Guy Cardwell, *The Man Who Was Mark Twain: Images and Ideologies* (New Haven, Conn.: Yale University Press, 1991).

CHAPTER 1

1. Olivia Langdon Clemens, commonplace book, 1863–71, 18. Mark Twain Papers, Bancroft Library, University of California, Berkeley. Subsequent references to this book will be documented internally.

2. Letter, Mary Ann Lewis, from Lenox, New York, to Olivia Lewis Langdon, in Enfield, New York, September 1, 1836, Chemung County Historical Society.

3. The author wishes to thank the Mark Twain Foundation for permission to quote from Olivia Langdon Clemens's papers.

4. The Elmira-Hartford connection has yet to be fully explored. Certainly Isabella Hooker's letters imply a long-standing familiarity with Elmira people, and Gretchen Sharlow has pointed out to me a January 26, 1863 letter from Isabella Hooker to her husband John in which she mentions that Jervis Langdon is a "cousin by marriage." The letter is owned by the Stowe-Day Library.

5. Isabella Beecher Hooker, letter to John Hooker, July 15 [and 16] 1860. Quoted in Jeanne Boydston, Mary Kelley, and Anne Margolis, eds., *The Limits of Sisterhood: The Beecher Sisters on Women's Rights and Woman's Sphere* (Chapel Hill: University of North Carolina Press, 1988), 107.

6. Letters, Alice Hooker Day to Isabella Hooker, Isabella Hooker Collection, Stowe-Day Library, Harriet Beecher Stowe Center, Hartford, Connecticut. Subsequent references to these letters will be documented

internally. The author wishes to thank the Stowe-Day Library for permission to quote from Alice Hooker Day's letters.

7. Edward Young, *Night Thoughts*, ed. Stephen Cornford (Cambridge University Press, 1989), 4. Subsequent references, including line references to the poem, will be documented internally.

8. Boydston, Kelley, and Margolis, eds., *Limits of Sisterhood*, 96.

9. Olivia Langdon to Alice Hooker, May 26, 1867, Clemens Family Letters, Mark Twain Memorial, Hartford, Connecticut. The author wishes to thank the memorial for permission to quote from unpublished materials.

10. Gleason received her M.D. in 1851, becoming one of four women in the United States to hold the degree. Jane B. Donegan, *"Hydropathic Highway to Health": Women and the Water-Cure in Antebellum America* (Westport, Conn.: Greenwood, 1986), 45.

11. Olivia Langdon Letters, November 30, 1878, MTM.

12. "Elmira's First Library," by William H. Arnold, county historian. Chemung County Historical Society, Vertical File, Library-Mechanics, 250–075. Also *New York Libraries*, published quarterly by the University of the State of New York, 10, no. 6 (February 1927): 187.

13. "Catalogue of Books Belonging to the Elmira Mechanics Library, 1843," Chemung County Historical Society.

14. "First Free Library: A Part of the Park Church Home," clipping dated January 9, 1899 (no other publication data available). Chemung County Historical Society, Vertical File Library-Mechanics, 250–075. Elmira had a large camp holding Confederate prisoners during the Civil War, and the town had many social problems associated with the influx of an artificially inflated population. Thievery was common.

15. Archives of the Park Church, Elmira, New York. My thanks to Gretchen Sharlow, director of the Center for Mark Twain Studies at Elmira College and chairperson of the Park Church Heritage Committee for these and other statistics. According to Ms. Sharlow, some seventy-five of the books remaining bear Thomas K. Beecher's initials, and two were donated by Olivia Langdon Clemens.

16. By languages I refer to the specialized sublanguages characteristic of many professions, one aspect of what Mikhail Bahktin calls "heteroglossia."

17. *Elmira Daily Advertiser*, January 1, 1866: 4.

18. Frederick Hall is listed as one of the proprietors of Hall Brothers Books in the 1860 Elmira Directory. According to the *Elmira Saturday Review* of July 30, 1870, the store had been established in 1842 by Frank Hall, who turned it over to his brothers Frederick, Charles, and Robert, in 1859 (p. 8). Frederick's name occurs throughout Olivia Lewis's diary as

one of the many friends of the Langdon seniors who floated in and out of their always-hospitable house. In January 1867 Hall Brothers advertised Luise Mühlbach's series of historical novels about Frederick the Great; *Elmira Daily Advertiser*, January 28, 1867: 4. *The Wept of Wishton Wish*, *The Draytons and Davenants*, and *Kitty Trevalyn's Diary*, all listed in the back of Olivia Lewis's diary under the heading "Books Read in 1867," were also sold there.

19. Hall Estate – four account books, no date, box 15, Chemung County Historical Society.

20. See, for example, a notice for a science lecture by a Professor Richards, which details the demonstrations to be given and concludes, "The innate beauty of the lecture alone should draw a full house, apart from the experiments, which render it perfectly ravishing and enticing" (*Popular Science*, March 11, 1869): 3.

21. As I indicated in note 6 in the Introduction, evidence suggests that the renovations to the house were even more extensive than Olivia Lewis Langdon's diary indicates. The Langdons seem to have acquired the Ely property in two lots; a section of land in 1862, and more land and the house later, probably in 1865. See newspaper item (undated) on the razing of the Langdon mansion in 1939 (Langdon file, Chemung County History Society, Elmira, N.Y.), and the deed for the November 1, 1862 purchase of land from Martha Ely (Chemung Deeds, 44, p. 3, Chemung County Courthouse, Elmira). My thanks to Gretchen Sharlow for sending me a copy of this deed.

22. S. Edward Rose, "Beginnings of the Railroad: Erie, Lackawanna, Tioga Division, EC&N," *Chemung County Historical Journal* 1, no. 4 (June 1957): 319–29.

23. *Elmira Daily Advertiser*, Notices of Erie and North Central railroad routes, March 20, 1869.

24. Ely Hall had a capacity of fourteen hundred people; the new opera house one of twenty-five hundred. *Elmira Daily Advertiser*, April 15, 1867.

25. *Elmira Weekly Gazette*, March 28, 1867, Steele Memorial Library, Elmira, N.Y.

26. *Elmira Weekly Gazette*, October 30, 1868, Opera House Lecture Series.

27. Louis J. Budd, ed., *Mark Twain: Collected Tales, Sketches, Speeches, and Essays, 1852–1890* (New York: Library of America, 1992), 964–6.

28. At this point Clemens thought he was going to have to return to California, where he had been the previous year. To his relief the trip was canceled.

29. Albert Bigelow Paine, *Mark Twain, A Biography* (New York: Harper, 1912), 3 vols.; vol. 1, 375.

CHAPTER 2

1. *Saturday Evening Review*, Elmira, New York, March 13, 1869: 5.
2. Sherwood Cummings, *Mark Twain and Science: Adventures of a Mind* (Baton Rouge: Louisiana State University Press, 1988).
3. Barbara Wiggins Taylor, "Education in the Life of Olivia Langdon Clemens to 1870," Master's thesis, Elmira College, 1991.
4. *Annual Catalogue of Officers and Pupils of the Elmira Seminary, Chemung County, New York for the Year Ending 30 September 1851* (New York: Baker, Godwin, 1851), Elmira College Archives.
5. In 1902 Susan Langdon Crane established an experimental dairy at Quarry Farm in cooperation with the American Association of Medical Milk Commission's drive to establish standards for clean milk. Until 1919, it was the only farm in the area to produce certified milk. One wonders how influential Crane's early education in science was to her decision to embark on this project. See Sharlow, *Love to All the Jolly Household*.
6. Taylor, "Education," 31–41.
7. On September 8, 1885 she recorded in her diary that "I began yesterday to show Jean [her youngest child, then five years old] something about insects – we went out and got a grasshopper, but it jumped about so in the glass where we put it that she could not see it very well. I did not want her to kill it, because I cannot get away from the feeling that it must greatly blunt a child's sensibility to allow it to kill the little creatures. . . . [later] I got one or two insects that killed themselves in the light of the lamp . . . I told her we would find what dead insects we could . . . and examine them."

   Though this search led to the enthusiastic young scientist's arraying a supply of dead flies on her mother's breakfast plate, Olivia Clemens remained concerned that her daughters understand the physical universe as well as their culture's languages and arts. Coming from a family and town that valued scientific investigation, she carried her early interests well into her adult life. Olivia Langdon Clemens Diary, September 8, 1885, MTP. The diary is not paginated. The author is grateful to the Mark Twain Papers for permission to quote from Olivia Langdon Clemens's unpublished materials.
8. See, for instance, his letter of December 31, 1868, in which he told Langdon that whereas the old year "found me a waif, floating at random upon the sea of life," the new year, because of her presence, found him with "a home that is priceless, a refuge from all the cares & ills of life, in that warm heart of yours." (*MTL* 2: 370). Also see chapter 7, "The Imagery of Protection," in Susan K. Harris's *Mark Twain's Escape from*

Time: A Study of Patterns and Images (Columbia: University of Missouri Press, 1982), 115–36.

9. In *Shaping Written Knowledge: The Genre and Activity of the Experimental Article in Science* (Madison: University of Wisconsin Press, 1988), Charles Bazerman traces the development of the scientific report in the *Philosophical Transactions of the Royal Society of London* between 1665 and 1800. By 1800, he demonstrates, the focus of scientific writing was beginning to shift from the experiences of the experimenter – i.e., the personal history of the scientist's manipulations of the materials being investigated – to investigation itself. One result of such a shift was to deemphasize the role of human subjectivity, not to speak of human manipulation, in the conduct of experiments and interpretations of results. See especially chapter 3, "Reporting the Experiment," 59–70. In *Science as Writing* (New Haven, Conn.: Yale University Press, 1992), David Locke comments extensively on the relationship between the objects of scientific discourse (what is being investigated) and the discourse itself.

10. See the reprint of this report in John C. Burnham, ed., *Science in America: Historical Selections* (New York: Holt, Rinehart & Winston, 1971), 170–85.

11. Robert V. Bruce, *The Launching of Modern American Science, 1846–1876* (Ithaca, N.Y.: Cornell University Press, 1987), 118. Subsequent references to this book will be documented internally.

12. *Popular Science Monthly,* 1, no. 1 (May 1872).

13. *American Journal of Science,* 46, nos. 136 and 137 (1868).

14. *Popular Science Monthly,* 1, no. 1 (May 1872): 115.

15. *Popular Science Monthly,* 1, no. 1 (May 1872): 114.

16. Albert B. Helmkamp, "The Elmira Academy, 1836–1859: Private Venture in Education," *Chemung County Historical Journal,* 1, no. 2 (December 1955): 74.

17. "Course of Instruction," *Elmira Female College Catalogue,* 1868, 20–1, Elmira College Archives. Elmira College was in fact progressive in its integration of science courses with a traditional liberal-arts curriculum; even after the Civil War, most institutions of higher education resisted the introduction of science into their core curricula. Hartford's Trinity College, older than Elmira but similar in size, was more like the large eastern universities in segregating science courses into special tracks: students of 1867-8 could elect to take a bachelor of science degree "in one of the following branches: viz.; Differential and Integral Calculus; Practical Astronomy; Analytical and Agricultural Chemistry; Geology and Minerology; Natural History; or Civil Engineering." (*Trinity College Catalogue, 1867–68* [Hartford: Church Press, 1867]: 23-4, Trinity College Archives, Watkinson Library.) Harvard's Lawrence Scientific School, which also constituted a separate track within the university and which

was for many years understaffed, underfunded, and woefully unrespected by its host institution, had nevertheless become a model for American scientific education; the writers of Elmira College's *Callisophia* remarked that the Academy of Science, with its library, museum, observatory, and discussion groups, would become "a kind of 'Lawrence Scientific School' for Elmira" (*Callisophia*, 1, no. 3 (July-August 1860): 4, Elmira College Archives).

18. Dr. Julius Adolph Stockhardt (professor in the Royal Academy of Agriculture at Tharand, and royal inspector of medicine in Saxony), *The Principles of Chemistry, Illustrated by Simple Experiments*, translated from the fifth German Edition by C. H. Peirce, M.D. (London: Henry G. Bohn, 1859).

19. The *Elmira College Catalogue* for 1867-8 lists Stockhardt's chemistry text as the one used in its collegiate department. Wells's textbook on natural philosophy, described in note 20 in this chapter, is also listed. Since Darius Ford, Olivia's tutor, also taught science at the college, and since both books are adaptable for home use, it is reasonable to assume that these were Langdon's texts. Elmira College Archives.

20. Stockhardt's text is especially clear on descriptions and directives. It describes a "common apothecaries' balance" for instance, as consisting of "a brass or steel lever (beam), with arms of equal length, through the centre of which passes a steel wedge-shaped axis, resting on a hardened plate, so that the beam, to the extremities of which the pans are attached, may easily vibrate. It is essential that the axis should be in the right place in the beam, a little *above* its centre of gravity, as in Fig. 1." (22). Similarly, David A. Wells's *Natural Philosophy; For the Use of Schools, Academies, and Private Students*, 15th edition, revised (New York: Ivison, Phinney, Blakeman, 1865) gives clear directions for finding the specific gravity of various substances: "Suppose we take five vessels, each of which would contain exactly one hundred grains of water, and fill them respectively with spirits, ice, water, iron, and quicksilver. The following differences in weight will be found: – The vessel filled with spirits would weigh 80 grains; with water, 100 grains; with iron, 750 grains; with quicksilver, 1,350 grains. Water having been selected as the standard . . . the question to be settled is simply this: How much lighter than water are spirits and ice, and how much heavier than water are iron and quicksilver; or, in other words, how many times is 100 contained in 80, 90, 750, and 1,350? The weights of the different substances filling the vessel are, therefore, to be divided by 100, the weight of the water" (38).

21. William S. W. Ruschenberger, *Report of the Condition of the Academy of Natural Sciences of Philadelphia* (Philadelphia, 1876), 40. As quoted in Bruce, *Modern Science*, 35–6.

22. "The Elmira Academy of Sciences, Brief History of its Origin and Operations," article from the Elmira history and directory, 1868, Elmira College Archives; Eva Taylor, "Elmira Academy of Science," *Chemung County Historical Journal*, 16, no. 4 (June 1971): 2037. Also see Gilbert Meltzer, *The Beginnings of Elmira College* (Elmira, N.Y.: Elmira College, 1941): 73–9.

23. City of Elmira directory, 1860; *Elmira Daily Advertiser*, Thursday, March 11, 1869, "City and Neighborhood" column. With Robert Collingwood, presumably his brother, Francis Collingwood also seems to have sold watches and jewelry and to have been an agent for Singer sewing machines.

24. *Charter, Constitution and By-Laws of the Elmira Academy of Science, with a List of the Members, Etc. 1897. Organized June 22, 1861* (Elmira, N.Y.: Gazette, 1897), Chemung County Historical Society. Adelle Gleason, a physician, was the daughter of doctors Silas and Rachel Gleason, who ran the Water Cure. The women listed in 1897 are not mentioned in documents relating to the 1860s; presumably they were among the next generation.

25. Both Collingwood and Gregg noted that a society such as theirs could not expect original investigation, and most of the members' research does seem to have been conducted in the library rather than in the field. Despite the second-hand research, the style with which it was reported mimicked scientific "objectivity." The "Chairman on Natural History, Dr. Murdoch," the *Callisophia* records, "discussed the question. . . . 'The change of the shore water mark on the Gulf of Mexico, as to whether the land had risen or the water had lowered.' It was the Chairman's view that the shore had been elevated, since the amount of water on the earth never changes. The elevation is caused by sediment, brought down by the rivers, and washed up by the ocean. It has been found by actual experiment that the Ganges, every sixty days, brings down solid matter, sufficient to form 60 pyramids, of 10 acres base, and 500 feet high. By boring 400 feet at the delta, remains of inland animals were found." *Callisophia*, 1, no. 4 (September–October 1860): 5.

26. "The Elmira Academy of Science," article from *Elmira History and Directory*, 1868, Elmira College Archives.

27. An equatorial telescope was mounted on two axes rather than one, enabling it to be revolved so that it could follow a star's path; as a contemporary textbook notes, the "heavenly body" in view can thus "be examined leisurely and with care." Transit telescopes, in contrast, were fixed in stone so that extremely accurate readings of sidereal time could be computed on the sidereal, or star-time, clock.

28. Both Sherwood Cummings and Hamlin Hill have discussed this piece, but it is worth going over once more as an example of Twain's critique

of scientific thinking. See Cummings, *Mark Twain and Science*, 26. Also see Hamlin Hill, "Mark Twain's 'Brace of Brief Lectures on Science,' " *New England Quarterly* 34 (1961): 228–39.

29. Mark Twain, "A Brace of Brief Lectures on Science," in Budd, ed., *Collected Tales*, 528–38. Subsequent references to this sketch will be documented internally.

30. Cummings, *Mark Twain and Science*, 12; and Hill, "'Brief Lectures,' " 239.

31. Charles Boysett, "Science and the Moral Order," *Galaxy*, 17 (January 1874): 130, quoted in Cummings, *Mark Twain and Science*, 6.

32. Mark Twain, "Science vs. Luck," in Budd, ed., *Collected Tales*, 452–4.

33. Mark Twain, "Some Learned Fables for Good Old Boys and Girls," in Budd, ed., *Collected Tales*, 611–31.

34. William Gibson, ed., *Mark Twain: The Mysterious Stranger* (Berkeley and Los Angeles: University of California Press, 1969), 331.

CHAPTER 3

1. In *The Book of Love: Writers and Their Love Letters* (New York: Simon & Schuster, 1992), Cathy N. Davidson categorizes some of the major features love letters share and discusses some of the functions they serve. I read this book well after finishing this chapter, and was interested to see how easily Davidson's taxonomy could be read into Clemens's letters, especially her discussion of love letters as performances.

2. Paine, *Mark Twain: A Biography*, vol. 1, 377–8.

3. Margaret Sanborn, *Mark Twain: The Bachelor Years* (New York: Doubleday, 1990), 200–1.

4. Andrew Hoffman, "Mark Twain and Homosexuality," *American Literature*, 67, no. 1 (March 1995): 27. In addition to (and probably more important than) its goal of destabilizing our conception of Twain's sexual orientations, Hoffman's article highlights our ignorance of nineteenth-century sexual concepts and practices. Answers to some of the questions he raises about male sexuality in the antebellum West could radically revise our understanding of frontier culture.

5. Isabella Hooker to Mary and Alice Hooker, September 15, 1867, Isabella Beecher Hooker Collection, Stowe-Day Library.

6. This may be worth a note, or it may not, but the more I read Jervis Langdon's April 2 letter to Clemens, the more I wonder about it. My reason tells me that the tone that bothers me results from Langdon's facetiousness and from the fact that he was suffering from stomach cancer at the time that he wrote – and that his pain was not conducive to a graceful epistolary style. I also dislike the current practice of reading

peculiarly twentieth-century concerns back into the interpretation of other centuries' values. Still, I wonder if there is a connection between the father's "love" and the daughter's long adolescent illness.

7. I wish to thank Professor Mary de Jong, of Pennsylvania State University, Shenango campus, for allowing me access to her unpublished paper "The Language of the Heart," presented at the "Hymns and Sermons" session of the American Literature Association Convention in Baltimore, Maryland, May 27–30, 1993.

8. Carol Christ, "Victorian Masculinity and the Angel in the House," in Martha Vicinus, ed., *A Widening Sphere: Changing Roles of Victorian Women* (Bloomington: Indiana University Press, 1977), 146–62.

9. Notes to the University of California Press edition of Clemens's letter give the source of these lines as letter 4, book 1, of Patmore's "Faithful for Ever," the third part of the verse narrative. In fact they occur at the end of letter 5. In some editions this section is titled merely "Frederick To His Mother."

10. Nina Baym, *Novels, Readers, and Reviewers: Responses to Fiction in Antebellum America* (Ithaca, N.Y.: Cornell University Press, 1984), chapter 3 and throughout.

11. DeLancey Ferguson, *Mark Twain: Man and Legend* (New York: Bobbs-Merrill, 1943); and Bradford A. Booth, "Mark Twain's Comments on Holmes's *Autocrat*," *American Literature* 21 (1950): 456–63.

12. The University of California Press edition of Clemens's letters quotes from a letter of Dickinson's that characterizes Clemens as a "vulgar boor" and professes not to understand why Langdon chose to marry him (*MTL* 3: 66, n2).

CHAPTER 4

1. Judith Fetterley, *The Resisting Reader: A Feminist Approach to American Fiction* (Bloomington: Indiana University Press, 1978). See especially "Introduction: On the Politics of Literature," xi–xxvi.

2. Alan Gribben, *Mark Twain's Library: A Reconstruction* (Boston: Hall, 1980), 2 vols.; vol. 1, 189.

3. Charles Dickens, *Dombey and Son*, in *The Works of Charles Dickens* (New York: Collier, 1911), 25 vols.; vol. 2, 693.

4. In *The Reproduction of Mothering: Psychoanalysis and the Sociology of Gender* (Berkeley and Los Angeles: University of California Press, 1978), Nancy Chodorow uses the psychoanalytic study of object relations to demonstrate how modes of parenting, especially by mothers, influence the development of boys into men protective of sharply delineated

ego-boundaries, and of girls into women able and willing to psychologically project themselves into others. See especially summarizing pp. 165–8. The anthology *Gender and Reading: Essays on Readers, Texts, and Contexts*, edited by Elizabeth A. Flynn and Patrocinio P. Schweickart (Baltimore: Johns Hopkins University Press, 1986), contains many essays focusing on the connections between gender and reading behavior.

5. Mikhail Bakhtin, *Rabelais and His World*, translated by Helene Iswolsky (Bloomington: Indiana University Press, 1984), 78–96.

6. Nathaniel Hawthorne, *The Marble Faun*, Richard H. Rupp, ed. (Indianapolis: Bobbs-Merrill, 1971), 40.

7. Olivia Langdon Clemens Diary, 1885–1902, June 7, 1885, Mark Twain Memorial.

8. See, for instance, "Fenian Arsenal Discovered in Jersey City," *Elmira Daily Advertiser*, January 6, 1866. The *Advertiser*, like other newspapers of the period, followed Fenian activities on a daily basis.

9. Martin Purtell, "Chemung County's Irish: The Master Builders," *Chemung County Historical Journal*, 1, no. 3 (March 1956): 99–105.

10. "Prison Association of New York," *Elmira Daily Advertiser*, January 13, 1866.

11. *Saturday Evening Review*, no. 10 (May 15, 1869): 3, report of meetings of the Chemung County Medical Society; "Ante-Natal Murder," editorial, *Saturday Evening Review*, no. 12 (May 29, 1869): 4. This latter is cast as a nativist diatribe against American abortions in light of immigrants' high birth rates.

12. We may be able to better understand this shaping feature of Twain's career by adapting a paradigm originally developed by Edwin Ardener, a cultural anthropologist, to examine the ideational relationship between men and women among the Bakweri of Cameroon, West Africa. In "Belief and the Problem of Women" and "The Problem Revisited," both in *The Voice of Prophecy and Other Essays*, Malcolm Chapman, ed. (New York: Blackwell, 1989), 72–85 and 127–33, Ardener suggests that whereas Bakweri men, traditionally anthropologists' chief informants, imaged the women of their tribe as beyond the pale, part of the "wild" that was literally beyond the compounds where the men passed most of their days, the women, when queried, were able to articulate a much more complex image of themselves as specifically and integrally women, living "as women in the men's wild, as well as partly within the men's world inside the village fence" (13). Noting in his first article that "we are all lay figures in someone else's play" (14), in his second article Ardener elaborates his insights that, first, the boundary lines that all human communities construct are perceived according to subgroups' locations in respect to them; and second, that dominant subgroups often

186

perceive "muted," that is, nonarticulated, social structures as "null," as backgrounds lacking interest or significance (24). Most important for our purposes here, Ardener points out that "all world-structures [i.e., group constructions of reality] are totalitarian in tendency" and that "*Dominance* occurs when one structure blocks the power of actualization of the other, so that it has no 'freedom of action' " (25).

Although introducing a paradigm from structural anthropology may seem unnecessarily esoteric, it should be useful in examining Mark Twain's reading and writing strategies, first, because it helps us move away from the illuminating but ultimately limiting binary opposites through which he is customarily viewed, and second, because without resorting to binary oppositions, it nevertheless helps us understand some of the complexities of his much-noted dualism.

13. Budd, ed., *Collected Tales*, 644–60. Subsequent references to this volume will be documented internally.

14. Of course "Facts," like all Twain's work, can be seen from a variety of angles. In *Sentimental Twain: Samuel Clemens in the Maze of Moral Philosophy* (Philadelphia: University of Pennsylvania Press, 1994), Gregg Camfield explicates it within the context of Twain's negotiations between utilitarian, Calvinist, and sentimental discourses about the conscience. See especially 116–21.

15. Which it did for twentieth-century critics if not for nineteenth-century readers. Traditionally, "1601" has been seen as pornographic. Recently, J. D. Stahl has given a much more reasoned reading of it in *Mark Twain, Culture and Gender: Envisioning America Through Europe* (Athens: University of Georgia Press, 1994), 55–65.

16. Budd, ed., *Collected Tales*, 661–6.

17. Late in his life Twain would again write about women's sexual desire. In part, he was writing out of a long tradition of viewing women's sexuality as insatiable and hence threatening. At the same time, his writings suggest that he may have begun to see that women were full sexual beings. If so, I suspect that Langdon's own sexuality was instrumental in his education. As Skandera-Twombley's work suggests, we are moving toward the critical and biographical moment when we will be able to acknowledge Langdon's awareness of her own sexuality and examine the effect this had on Clemens.

18. In *The Heroines of Shakespeare: Their Moral, Poetical, and Historical Characters* (Philadelphia: Potter, n.d.), Anna Jameson treats Portia as "uniting in herself . . . all the noblest and most loveable qualities that ever met together in a woman" (41). Widely read and quoted, Jameson's works on female artists and characters functioned as bulwarks of the establishment view of women as innately and necessarily "feminine" – femininity was

of the utmost importance to Jameson – and also as capable of much successful activity within that sphere. Olivia Langdon copied passages from several of Jameson's works into her commonplace book.

19. Sander L. Gilman, "Mark Twain and the Diseases of the Jews," *American Literature*, 65 (1993): 95–116.

20. Mark Twain, *The Innocents Abroad* (New York: Signet, 1966), 158.

21. The parody occurs in one of Twain's "letters" written for the Virginia City, Nevada, *Enterprise* in 1863, where he is parodying a "Mr. Sterns," presumably a delegate to the Nevada legislature. See Henry Nash Smith, ed., *Mark Twain of the Enterprise: Newspaper Articles and Other Documents, 1862–1864* (Berkeley and Los Angeles: University of California Press, 1957), 94.

22. Luise Mühlbach, *Berlin and Sans-Souci, or, Frederick the Great and His Friends*, translated from the German by Mrs. Chapman Coleman and her daughters (New York: Appleton, 1867), 471.

23. Dixon Wecter, ed., *Mark Twain to Mrs. Fairbanks* (San Marino, Calif.: Huntington Library, 1949), 208.

24. Mark Twain, "A General Reply," *Galaxy*, vol x, no. 5 (November 1870): 732–4. Reprinted in Budd, ed., *Collected Tales*, 487.

25. Though this edition was published in 1856, the copy Clemens read was inscribed in 1870 and was probably a wedding present. It is owned by the Mark Twain Memorial in Hartford, which possesses several history and reference books that must have been wedding gifts.

26. Thomas Carlyle, *The French Revolution: A History* (New York: Harper & Brothers, 1856), 2 vols.; vol. 1, 13.

27. Over the years Clemens also wrote in other copies of Carlyle. See Gribben, *Mark Twain's Library*, vol. 1, 128.

28. Of course this attitude is just that: an attitude, a pose. As students of Clemens's biography know, he also professed great respect for those who, like Anson Burlingame in the mid-1860s, offered helpful advice. See *MTL* 1: 345–6.

29. "Female Suffrage: Views of Mark Twain," in Budd, ed., *Mark Twain*, 214–23. Subsequent page numbers will be documented internally.

30. Though none of this sounds remarkable to readers steeped in modernist and postmodernist writing, it was uncommon among mainstream writers of the nineteenth century. Most, like today's professional columnists, orchestrated characters' voices from an authoritative center. In contrast, Twain often eschewed a controlling authorial presence, moving between subject positions without subordinating them to a unifying authorial consciousness. Like his episodic plots, his narrative ideation often lacks centricity.

31. William M. Thackeray, *English Humorists of the Eighteenth Century*, in *The*

Works of William Makepeace Thackeray (London: Smith, Elder, 1869), 24 vols.; vol. 19, 156.

32. Alan Gribben has noted these marginal comments, as well as earlier critical work commentary on them. See Gribben, *Mark Twain's Library*, 697-8.

CHAPTER 5

1. Charles Dudley Warner to George Warner, February 14, 1870, Katharine S. Day Collection, Stowe-Day Library. According to Warner the house and furniture were worth at least $40,000.

2. See especially his letter from Paris, Ill., December 31, 1871, which contains a description of a church service that must have fed directly into the writing of *Tom Sawyer* (*MTL* 4: 527-30).

3. OLC is discussing a "Mrs. Warner" here, but it is not clear from the letter whether she is referring to Lilly or to Susan Warner. Both were neighbors and friends.

4. Dixon Wecter, ed., *Mark Twain to Mrs. Fairbanks*, 160.

5. The Reverend Joseph Hopkins Twichell was the minister of Hartford's Asylum Hill Congregational Church and a close friend of Samuel and Olivia Clemens.

6. Elisabeth (Lilly) Gillette Warner to George H. Warner, June 3, 1872, MTP.

7. Francis Goodwin II, *The Monday Evening Club of Hartford, Connecticut: Its Members & the Titles of Papers Read at Their Meetings, 1869-1970* (Hartford, Conn.: Privately printed, 1970).

8. Lilly Warner to George Warner, November 15, 1871, KSD Coll., Stowe-Day. Feelings about the club were not all tranquil. Apparently George Warner had never been invited to join, and in this letter his wife voices her resentment of the slight.

9. Dixon Wecter, ed., *Love Letters of Mark Twain* (New York: Harper, 1949), 173-4.

10. Ibid., 172-3.

11. Kenneth R. Andrews, *Nook Farm: Mark Twain's Hartford Circle* (Seattle: University of Washington Press, 1950), 101.

12. Mark Twain, "A Mysterious Visit," in Budd, ed., *Collected Tales*, 341-4.

13. Pottier and Stymus was an interior decorating house in New York City that catered to the Victorian upper class. Olivia Lewis Langdon's diary mentions using them for the renovations for the Langdon house in Elmira.

14. Langdon's references are to the family business and to her brother Charles, who had assumed control after their father's death.
15. Langdon mentions holding $200 of her mother's and £43 of Pamela's.
16. Mark Twain Collection (#6314), Clifton Waller Barrett Library, Special Collections Department, University of Virginia Library. The author wishes to thank the University of Virginia for permission to quote from this letter.
17. Lilly Warner to George Warner, November 14, 1871, MTP.
18. Lilly Warner to George Warner, January 14, 1873, MTP.

WORKS CITED

PRIMARY WORKS

Twain, Mark

Mark Twain: Collected Tales, Sketches, Speeches, and Essays, 1852–1890, ed. Louis J. Budd. New York: Library of America, 1992.

Mark Twain's Letters, Volume 1, 1853–1866, ed. Edgar Marquess Branch, Michael B. Frank, and Kenneth M. Sanderson. Berkeley and Los Angeles: University of California Press, 1988.

Mark Twain's Letters, Volume 2, 1867–1868, ed. Harriet Elinor Smith, Richard Bucci, and Lin Salamo. Berkeley and Los Angeles: University of California Press, 1990.

Mark Twain's Letters, Volume 3, 1869, ed. Victor Fischer, Michael B. Frank, and Dahlia Armon. Berkeley and Los Angeles: University of California Press, 1992.

Mark Twain's Letters, Volume 4, 1870–1871, ed. Victor Fischer, Michael B. Frank, and Lin Salamo. Berkeley and Los Angeles: University of California Press, 1995.

Twain, Mark. *The Innocents Abroad.* New York: Signet, 1966.

Wecter, Dixon, ed. *The Love Letters of Mark Twain.* New York: Harper, 1949.

Wecter, Dixon, ed. *Mark Twain and Mrs. Fairbanks.* San Marino, Calif.: Huntington Library, 1949.

SELECTED SECONDARY WORKS

Andrews, Kenneth R. *Nook Farm: Mark Twain's Hartford Circle.* Seattle: University of Washington Press, 1950.

Ardener, Edwin. "Belief and the Problem of Women." In *The Voice of Prophecy and Other Essays*, ed. Malcom Chapman. New York: Blackwell, 1989, 72–85.

"The Problem Revisited." In *The Voice of Prophecy and Other Essays*, ed. Malcom Chapman. New York: Blackwell, 1989, 127–33.

Bakhtin, Mikhail M. *Rabelais and His World*, trans. Helene Iswolsky. Bloomington: Indiana University Press, 1984.

Baym, Nina. *Novels, Readers, and Reviewers: Responses to Fiction in Antebellum America.* Ithaca, N.Y.: Cornell University Press, 1984.

Bazerman, Charles. *Shaping Written Knowledge: The Genre and Activity of the Experimental Article in Science.* Madison: University of Wisconson Press, 1988.

Booth, Bradford A. "Mark Twain's Comments on Holmes's *Autocrat.*" *American Literature* 21 (1950): 456–63.

Boydston, Jeanne, Mary Kelley, and Anne Margolis, eds. *The Limits of Sisterhood: The Beecher Sisters on Women's Rights and Women's Sphere.* Chapel Hill: University of North Carolinia Press, 1988.

Boysett, Charles. "Science and the Moral Order." *Galaxy* 17 (1874): 130.

Bruce, Robert V. *The Launching of American Modern Science, 1846–1876.* Ithaca, N.Y.: Cornell University Press, 1987.

Burnham, John C., ed. *Science in America: Historical Selections.* New York: Holt, Rinehart & Winston, 1971.

Camfield, Gregg. *Sentimental Twain: Samuel Clemens in the Maze of Moral Philosophy.* Philadelphia: University of Pennsylvania Press, 1994.

Cardwell, Guy. *The Man Who Was Mark Twain: Images and Ideologies.* New Haven, Conn.: Yale University Press, 1991.

Carlyle, Thomas. *The French Revolution: A History*, ed. K. J. Fielding and David Sorensen. New York: Oxford University Press, 1989.

Chodorow, Nancy. *The Reproduction of Mothering: Psychoanalysis and the Sociology of Gender.* Berkeley and Los Angeles: University of California Press, 1978.

Christ, Carol. "Victorian Masculinity and the Angel in the House." In *A Widening Sphere: Changing Roles of Victorian Women*, ed. Martha Vicinus. Bloomington: Indiana University Press, 1977.

Cummings, Sherwood. *Mark Twain and Science: Adventures of a Mind.* Baton Rouge: Louisiana State University Press, 1988.

Davidson, Cathy N. *The Book of Love: Writers and Their Love Letters.* New York: Simon & Schuster, 1992.

de Jong, Mary. "The Language of the Heart." Paper presented as part of the session entitled "Hymns and Sermons in American Literature," American Literature Association Convention, Baltimore, Md., May 27–30, 1993.

Dickens, Charles. *Dombey and Son.* In *The Works of Charles Dickens.* New York: Collier, 1911. 25 vols.; vol. 2.

Donegan, Jane B. *"Hydropathic Highway to Health": Women and the Water-Cure in Antebellum America.* Westport, Conn.: Greenwood, 1986.

Ferguson, DeLancey. *Mark Twain: Man and Legend.* New York: Bobbs-Merrill, 1943.

Fetterley, Judith. *The Resisting Reader: A Feminist Approach to American Fiction.* Bloomington: Indiana University Press, 1978.

Flynn, Elizabeth A., and Patrocinio P. Schweickart, eds. *Gender and Reading: Essays on Readers, Texts, and Contexts.* Baltimore, Md.: Johns Hopkins University Press, 1986.

Gibson, William, ed. *Mark Twain: The Mysterious Stranger.* Berkeley and Los Angeles: University of California Press, 1969.

Gilman, Sander, L. "Mark Twain and the Diseases of the Jews." *American Literature,* 65 (1993): 95–116.

Goodwin, Francis II. *The Monday Evening Club of Hartford, Connecticut: Its Members and the Titles of Papers Read at Their Meetings, 1869–1970.* Hartford, Conn.: Privately printed, 1970.

Gribben, Alan. *Mark Twain's Library: A Reconstruction.* Boston: Hall, 1980. 2 vols.

Harris, Susan K. *Mark Twain's Escape from Time: A Study of Patterns and Images.* Columbia: University of Missouri Press, 1982.

Hawthorne, Nathaniel. *The Marble Faun,* ed. Richard H. Rupp. Indianapolis: Bobbs-Merrill, 1971.

Helmkamp, Albert B. "The Elmira Academy, 1836–1859: Private Venture in Education." *Chemung County Historical Journal,* 1, no. 2 (December 1955): 74.

Hill, Hamlin. "Mark Twain's 'Brace of Brief Lectures on Science.' " *New England Quarterly,* 34 (1961): 228–39.

Hoffman, Andrew Jay. "Mark Twain and Homosexuality." *American Literature,* 67, no. 1 (March 1995): 23–50.

Jameson, Anna. *The Heroines of Shakespeare: Their Moral, Poetical, and Historical Characters.* Philadelphia: Potter, n.d.

Locke, David. *Science as Writing.* New Haven, Conn.: Yale University Press, 1992.

Meltzer, Gilbert. *The Beginnings of Elmira College.* Elmira, N.Y.: Elmira College, 1941.

Mühlbach, Luise. *Berlin and San-Souci, or, Frederick the Great and His Friends,* trans. Mrs. Chapman Coleman and her daughters. New York: Appleton, 1867.

Paine, Albert Bigelow. *Mark Twain: A Biography.* New York: Harper, 1912. 3 vols.; vol. 1.

Patmore, Coventry. *The Angel in the House.* London: MacMillan, 1863.

Purtell, Martin. "Chemung County's Irish: The Master Builders." *Chemung County Historical Journal*, 1, no. 3 (1956): 99–105.

Rose, S. Edward. "Beginnings of the Railroad: Erie, Lackawanna, Tioga Division, EC&N." *Chemung County Historical Journal*, 1, no. 4 (June 1957): 319–29.

Ruschenberger, William S. W. *Report of the Condition of the Academy of Natural Sciences of Philadelphia.* Philadelphia, Academy of Natural Sciences, 1876.

Sanborn, Margaret. *Mark Twain: The Bachelor Years.* New York: Doubleday, 1990.

Sharlow, Gretchen. *"Love to All the Jolly Household:" A Study of the Cranes of Quarry Farm, Their Lives and Their Relationship with Mark Twain.* Master's thesis, Elmira College, 1991.

Skandera-Trombley, Laura E. *Mark Twain in the Company of Women.* Philadelphia: University of Pennsylvania Press, 1994.

Smith, Henry Nash, ed. *Mark Twain of the Enterprise: Newpaper Articles and Other Documents, 1862–1864.* Berkeley and Los Angeles: University of California Press, 1957.

Stahl, J. D. *Mark Twain, Culture and Gender: Envisioning America Through Europe.* Athens: University of Georgia Press, 1994.

Steinbrink, Jeffrey. *Getting To Be Mark Twain.* Berkeley and Los Angeles: University of California Press, 1991.

Stockhardt, Dr. Julius Adolph. *The Principles of Chemistry, Illustrated by Simple Experiments*, trans. from 5th German edition by C. H. Peirce, M.D. London: Henry G. Bohn, 1859.

Taylor, Barbara Wiggins. *Education in the Life of Olivia Langdon Clemens to 1870.* Master's thesis, Elmira College, 1991.

Thackeray, William M. *The Four Georges* and *English Humorists of the Eighteenth Century.* In *The Works of William Makepeace Thackeray.* London: Smith, Elder, 1869. 24 vols., 1869–86; vol. 19.

Towner, Ausburn. *A Brief History of Chemung County, New York.* New York: Barnes, 1907.

Trowbridge, John. "Note by the Editor, on the Progress of Science for the Year 1869." In *Annual of Scientific Discovery, Or, Year-Book of Facts in Science and Art, for 1870.* Boston: Gould & Lincoln, 1870, iii–xxii. Reprinted in *Science in America: Historical Selections*, ed. John C. Burnham. New York: Holt, Rinehart & Winston, 1971, 170–85.

Wells, David A. *Natural Philosophy; For the Use of Schools, Academies, and Private Students.* 15th revised edition. New York: Ivison, Phinney, Blakeman, 1865.

Willis, Resa. *Mark and Livy: The Love Story of Mark Twain and the Woman Who Almost Tamed Him.* New York: Atheneum, 1992.

Wright, Abner C. "Underground Railroad Activities in Elmira." *Chemung County Historical Journal,* 14, no. 1 (1968): 1755–7.

Youmans, E. L., ed. *Popular Science Monthly,* 1 (1872).

Young, Edward. *Night Thoughts,* ed. Stephen Cornford. Cambridge University Press, 1989.

ARCHIVES

Chemung County Historical Society Archives, Elmira, N.Y.

Elmira College Archives, Elmira, N.Y.

Isabella Hooker Collection. Stowe-Day Library, Harriet Beecher Stowe Center, Hartford, Conn.

Katharine S. Day Collection. Stowe-Day Library, Harriet Beecher Stowe Center, Hartford, Conn.

Langdon Family File. Chemung County Historical Society, Elmira, N.Y.

Mark Twain Memorial. Watkinson Library, Trinity College, Hartford, Conn.

Mark Twain Papers. Bancroft Library, University of California, Berkeley.

Park Street Church Archives, Elmira, N.Y.

Steele Memorial Library, Elmira, N.Y.

Trinity College Archives, Watkinson Library, Trinity College, Hartford, Conn.

INDEX

197

CAMBRIDGE STUDIES IN AMERICAN LITERATURE AND CULTURE

Continued from the front of the book